Listen,
Little Man!

WITHDRAWN

BOOKS BY WILHELM REICH

The Cancer Biopathy

Character Analysis

Early Writings: Volume One

Ether, God and Devil/Cosmic Superimposition

The Function of the Orgasm

The Invasion of Compulsory Sex-Morality

Listen, Little Man!

The Mass Psychology of Fascism

The Murder of Christ

Reich Speaks of Freud

Selected Writings

The Sexual Revolution

My God!

WILHELM REICH

Listen, Little Man!

TRANSLATED BY
Ralph Manheim

WITH ILLUSTRATIONS BY
William Steig

The Noonday Press
Farrar, Straus, and Giroux
New York

Library of Congress catalog card number: 73-87701

Published in Canada by HarperCollins*CanadaLtd*

Printed in the United States of America

Designed by Irving Perkins

Fifteenth printing, 1996

You sanctimonious philistines, who scoff at me!
What has your politics fed on
since you've been ruling the world?
On butchery and murder!

Charles de Coster, TILL ULENSPIEGEL

PREFACE

LISTEN, LITTLE MAN! is a human, not a scientific document. It was written in the summer of 1946 for the Archives of the Orgone Institute.* At the time there was no intention of publishing it. It reflects the inner turmoil of a scientist and physician who had observed the little man for many years and seen, first with astonishment, then with horror, what he *does to himself;* how he suffers, rebels, honors his enemies and murders his friends; how, wherever he acquires power "in the name of the people," he misuses it and transforms it into something more cruel than the tyranny he had previously suffered at the hands of upperclass sadists.

This appeal to the little man was a silent response to gossip and slander. When it was written, no one could foresee that a government agency charged with the safeguard of public health, in league with politicians and psychoanalytical careerists, would unleash an attack on orgone research. The decision to publish this appeal as a historical document was made in 1947, when the emotional plague conspired to kill orgone research (n.b., not to prove

* There are indications in the Archives of the Orgone Institute that *Listen, Little Man!* evolved between 1943 and 1946.—Ed.

ix

it unsound but to kill it by defamation). It was felt that the "common man" must learn what a scientist and psychiatrist actually is and what he, the little man, looks like to his experienced eye. He must be made acquainted with the reality which alone can counteract his ruinous craving for authority and be told very clearly what a grave *responsibility* he bears in everything he does, whether he is working, loving, hating, or just talking. He must learn how he gets to be a black or red fascist. Anyone who is fighting for the safeguard of life and the protection of our children must necessarily oppose red as well as black fascism. Not because the red fascists, like the black fascists in their day, have a murderous ideology but because they make cripples, puppets, and moral idiots of living healthy children; because they exalt the state over justice, lies over truth, and war over life; because children and the preservation of the life-force that is in them are the only hope we have left. An educator and physician knows only *one* allegiance: to the life-force in child and patient. If he is true to this allegiance, he will find simple answers to his political problems.

This appeal does not ask to be taken as a guide to life. It describes the emotional storms of a productive individual who loves life. It does not propose to convince or to win adherents. It sets forth experience as a painting sets forth a storm. It makes no plea for the reader's sympathy. It formulates no program. The scientist and thinker asks but one thing of the reader: a personal reaction such as poets and philosophers have always been assured of. It is a hard-working scientist's protest against the secret, unavowed design of the emotional plague to destroy him with poison arrows shot from a secure hiding place. It shows what the emotional plague is, how it functions and how it obstructs progress. It is also a profession of faith in the vast treasures that lie untapped in the depths of "human nature," ready to be utilized for the fulfillment of human hopes.

Those who are truly alive are kindly and unsuspecting in their human relationships and consequently endangered under present conditions. They assume that others think and act generously, kindly, and helpfully, in accordance with the laws of life. This natural attitude, fundamental to healthy children as well as to primitive man, inevitably represents a great danger in the struggle for a rational way of life as long as the emotional plague subsists, because the plague-ridden impute their own manner of thinking and acting to their fellow men. A kindly man believes that all men are kindly, while one infected with the plague believes that all men lie and cheat and are hungry for power. In such a situation the living are at an obvious disadvantage. When they give to the plague-ridden, they are sucked dry, then ridiculed or betrayed.

This has always been true. It is high time for the living to get tough, for toughness is indispensable in the struggle to safeguard and develop the life-force; this will not detract from their goodness, as long as they stand courageously by the truth. There is ground for hope in the fact that among millions of decent, hard-working people there are *only a few* plague-ridden individuals, who do untold harm by appealing to the dark, dangerous drives of the armored average man and mobilizing him for political murder. There is but one antidote to the average man's predisposition to plague: his own feeling for true life. The life-force does not seek power but demands only to play its full and acknowledged part in human affairs. It manifests itself through love, work, and knowledge.

Anyone who wants to safeguard the life-force from the emotional plague must learn to make at least as much use of the right of free speech that we enjoy in America for good ends as the emotional plague does for evil ones. Granted equal opportunity for expression, rationality is bound to win out in the end. That is our great hope.

Listen,
Little Man!

You're a "little man," a "common man"

THEY CALL YOU Little Man, or Common Man. They say your day has dawned, the "Age of the Common Man."

You don't say that, little man. *They* do, the vice presidents of great nations, the labor leaders, the repentant sons of the bourgeoisie, the statesmen and philosophers. They give you the future, but they ask no questions about your past.

You've inherited a terrible past. Your heritage is a burning diamond in your hand. That's what *I* have to tell you.

A doctor, a shoemaker, mechanic, or educator has to know his shortcomings if he is to do his work and earn his living. For several decades now you have been taking over, throughout the world. The future of the human race will depend on your thoughts and actions. But your teachers and masters don't tell you how you really think and what you really are; no one dares to confront you with the one truth that might make you the unswerving master of your fate. You are "free" in only one respect: free from the self-criticism that might help you to govern your own life.

I've never heard you complain: "You exalt me as the future master of myself and my world. But you don't tell me how a man becomes master of himself, and you don't tell me what's wrong with me, what's wrong with what I think and do."

You let the powerful demand power "for the little man." But you yourself are silent. You provide powerful men with more power or choose weak, malignant men to represent you. And you discover too late that you are always the dupe.

I understand you. Because time and time again I've seen you naked in body and soul, without your mask, political label, or national pride. Naked as a newborn babe, naked as a field marshal in his underclothes. I've heard you weep and lament; you've told me your troubles, laid bare your love and yearning. I know you and understand you. I'm going to tell you what you are, little man, because I really believe in your great future. Because the future undoubtedly belongs to you, take a look at yourself. See yourself as you really are. Hear what none of your leaders or spokesmen dares to tell you:

You're a "little man," a "common man." Consider the double meanings of these words "little" and "common". . .

Don't run away! Have the courage to look at yourself!

"By what right are you lecturing me?" I see the question in your frightened eyes. I hear it on your insolent tongue, little man. You are afraid to look at yourself, little man, you're afraid of criticism, and afraid of the power that is promised you. What use will you make of your power? You don't know. You're afraid to think that your self—the man you feel yourself to be—might someday be different from what it is now: free rather than cowed, candid rather than scheming; capable of loving, not like a thief in the night but in broad daylight. You despise yourself, little man. You say, "Who am I that I should have an opinion, govern my life, and call the world mine?" You're right: who are you to lay claim to your life? I will tell you who you are.

You differ from a great man in only one respect: the

great man was once a very little man, but he developed *one* important quality: he recognized the smallness and narrowness of his thoughts and actions. Under the pressure of some task which meant a great deal to him, he learned to see how his smallness, his pettiness, endangered his happiness. *In other words, a great man knows when and in what way he is a little man. A little man does not know he is little and is afraid to know.* He hides his pettiness and narrowness behind illusions of strength and greatness, *someone else's* strength and greatness. He's proud of his great generals but not of himself. He admires an idea he has not had, *not* one he has had. The less he understands something, the more firmly he believes in it. And the better he understands an idea, the less he believes in it.

Let me begin with the little man in myself.

For twenty-five years I've been speaking and writing in defense of your right to happiness in this world, condemning your inability to take what is your due, to secure what you won in bloody battles on the barricades of Paris and Vienna, in the American Civil War, in the Russian Revolution. Your Paris ended with Pétain and Laval, your Vienna with Hitler, your Russia with Stalin, and your America may well end in the rule of the Ku Klux Klan! You've been more successful in winning your freedom than in securing it for yourself and others. This I knew long ago. What I did not understand was why time and again, after fighting your way out of a swamp, you sank into a worse one. Then groping and cautiously looking about me, I gradually found out what has enslaved you: YOUR SLAVE DRIVER IS YOU YOURSELF. No one is to blame for your slavery but you yourself. *No one else,* I say!

That's news to you, isn't it? Your liberators tell you that

mercy of the little man. The little man doesn't want to hear the truth about himself. He doesn't want the great responsibility that has fallen to him, that is his whether he likes it or not. He wants to go on being a little man, or to become a little big man. He wants to get rich or become a party leader or head of the VFW or secretary of a society for moral uplift. But he does not want to assume responsibility for his work, for food supply, construction, mining, transportation, education, scientific research, administration, or what have you.

Only you yourself can be your liberator

The little man in me says:

"You have become a great man, known in Germany, Austria, Scandinavia, England, America, and Palestine. The Communists attack you. The 'saviors of cultural values' hate you. The sufferers from the emotional plague persecute you. You have written twelve books and 150 articles about the misery of life, the misery of the little man. Your work is taught at universities, other great, lonely men say you're a *very* great man. You are ranked among the giants of scientific thought. You have made the greatest discovery in centuries, for you have discovered cosmic life energy and the laws of living matter. You have provided an understanding of cancer. You told the truth. For that you have been hunted from country to country. You've earned a rest. Enjoy your success and your fame. In a few years your name will be on all lips. You've done enough. Take it easy. Devote yourself to your work on the functional law of nature."

That's what the little man in me says, because he's afraid of you, little man.

I was in close contact with you for many years, because I knew your life through my own and wanted to help you. I remained in contact with you, because I saw that I was indeed helping you and that you accepted my help willingly, often with tears in your eyes. Only very gradually did I come to see that you are capable of accepting help but not of defending it. I defended it and fought hard for you, in your stead. Then your leaders came and shattered my work. You followed them without a murmur. After that I remained in contact with you in the hope of finding a way to help you without being destroyed by you, either as your leader or as your victim. The little man in me a *single* master and become an *indiscriminate* slave, you must first kill the individual oppressor, the tsar for instance. You cannot commit such a political murder without revolutionary motives and a lofty ideal of freedom. Accordingly, you found a revolutionary freedom party under the leadership of a truly great man, let's say Jesus, Marx, Lincoln, or Lenin. This truly great man is dead serious about your freedom. If he wants practical results, he has to surround himself with little men, with helpers and executants, because the task is enormous and he can't handle it all by himself. Besides, you wouldn't understand him, you'd ignore him if he didn't gather little big men around him. Surrounded by little big men, he gains power for you, or a bit of truth, or a new and better faith. He writes testaments, issues laws to ensure freedom, counting on your help and serious willingness to help. He lifts you out of the social muck you had sunk into. In order to keep all the little big men together and not to forfeit your confidence, the truly great man is compelled, little by little, to sacrifice the greatness he had achieved in profound spiritual solitude, far from you and your daily tumult, yet in close contact with your life. In order to lead you, he must let you worship him as an unapproachable god. You would have no confidence in him if he went on being the simple man he was, if, for instance, he lived with a woman out of wedlock. Thus it is *you* who create your *new* master. Exalted to the rank of the new master, the great man loses his greatness, which consisted in integrity, simplicity, courage, and closeness to the realities of life. The little big men, who derive their prestige from the great man, take over the leading positions in finance, diplomacy, government, the arts and sciences—and you stay where you have

Little big man

been all along, *in the muck!* You continue to go about in rags for the sake of the "socialist future" or the "Third Reich." You continue to live in mud huts daubed with cow dung. But you're proud of your Palace of People's Culture. You're satisfied with the *illusion* that you hold power . . . Until the *next* war and the downfall of the *new* masters.

In far countries little men have closely studied your longing to be an indiscriminate slave. It has taught them how to become little big men with very little mental effort. These little men were not born in mansions, they rose from *your* ranks. They have gone hungry like you, suffered like you. And they have found a quicker way of changing masters. For a hundred years truly great thinkers made unstinting sacrifices, devoting their minds and lives to your freedom and well-being. The little men from your own ranks have found out that no such effort is needed. What truly great thinkers had achieved in a century of hardship and earnest thought they have managed to destroy in less than five years. Yes, the little men from your own ranks have found a shortcut—their method is more blatant and brutal. They tell you in so many words that you and your life, your children and family, count for nothing; that you are a feeble-minded flunky to be treated as it suits them. They promise you not individual but *national* freedom. They say nothing of self-respect but tell you to respect the state. They promise you not personal greatness but national greatness. Since "individual freedom" and "individual greatness" mean nothing to you, while "national freedom" and "national interest" stimulate your vocal cords in very much the same way as bones bring the water to a dog's mouth, the sound of these words makes you cheer. None of these little men pays the price that Giordano Bruno, Jesus, Karl Marx, or Lincoln had to pay for genuine freedom. They don't love you, little man, they despise you *because you despise yourself*. They know you through and through, much better than Rockefeller or the Tories know you. They know your worst weaknesses, as *you* ought to know them. They have sacrificed you to a symbol, and you have given them power over you. You yourself have raised up your masters and you go on supporting them although—or perhaps because—they have cast off all masks. They have told you plainly, "You are and always will be an inferior, incapable of responsibility." You call them guides or redeemers, and shout hurrah, hurrah.

Guides and redeemers

I'm afraid of you, little man, very much afraid, because the future of mankind depends on you. I'm afraid of you because your main aim in life is to escape —from yourself. You're sick, little man, very sick. It's not your fault; but it's your responsibility to get well. You'd have shaken off your oppressors long ago if you hadn't countenanced oppression and often given it your direct support. No police force in the world would have had the power to crush you if you had an ounce of self-respect in your daily life, if you were aware, really aware, that without you life could not go on for one hour. Has your liberator told you this? He called you "Workers of the World," but he didn't tell you that you and *you alone* are responsible for your life (and not for the honor of the fatherland).

You've got to realize that you have raised up your little men to be oppressors, and made martyrs of your truly great men; that you have crucified and stoned them, or let them starve; that you have never given a moment's thought to them or to what they have done for you; that you haven't the faintest idea who brought you the true benefits of your life.

"Before I trust you, I want to know where you stand."

When I tell you where I stand, you'll go running to the district attorney or the Committee on Un-American Activities or the FBI or the GPU or your favorite scandal sheet or the Ku Klux Klan or the various leaders of the world proletariat.

I am neither a white nor a black nor a red nor a yellow.

I am neither a Christian nor a Jew nor a Mohammedan nor a Mormon. I am neither a polygamist nor a homosexual nor an anarchist.

I embrace a woman because I love and desire her, not because I have a marriage certificate or because I'm sex-starved.

I don't beat children. I don't fish or hunt, even though I'm a good shot and enjoy shooting at targets. I don't play bridge and I don't give parties to air my ideas. If my ideas are sound, they'll air themselves.

I don't submit my work to any medical authority unless he understands it better than I do. And *I* decide who understands my discoveries and who doesn't.

I observe to the letter all laws that make sense but combat those that are obsolete or absurd. (Don't go running to the district attorney, little man! If he's an honest man he does the same.)

I want children and young people to enjoy physical love without hindrance.

I do not believe that to be religious in the best, authentic sense a man has to destroy his love life and mummify himself, body and soul.

I know that what you call "God" really exists, but not in the form you think; God is primal cosmic energy, the love in your body, your integrity, and your perception of the nature in you and outside of you.

If anyone, on any pretext whatsoever, tried to interfere with my work as a physician or educator, I'd throw him out. And if called into court, I'd ask him certain clear, simple questions that he'd be unable to answer without feeling ashamed for the rest of his life—because I'm a man who works, who knows what a human being is like inside, who knows that every human being has his worth, and who wants the world to be governed by *work* and not by opinions about work. I have my own opinion and I can distinguish lies from the truth, which I use as a tool every hour of the day, which I clean when I finish using it, and keep clean.

I'm afraid of you, little man, very much afraid. I haven't always been so. I myself was a little man, among millions of little men. Then I became a scientist and psychiatrist. I learned to see how very sick you are, and how dangerous in your sickness. I learned to see that it's your own psychic disorder and not any superior power outside you that holds you down—daily, hourly, even in the absence of external coercion. You'd have overcome the tyrants long ago if you had been inwardly alive and sound. In the past your oppressors sprang from the upper classes of society, but today they spring from your own ranks. They are even littler men than you, little man. They must be very little indeed to know your wretchedness from their own experience and on the basis of this knowledge to oppress you *more efficiently* and *more cruelly* than ever.

You have no eye, no feeling for the truly great man. His character, his suffering, his yearning, his fury, and his struggle in your behalf are foreign to you. You are unaware that men and women exist who are inherently incapable of oppressing and exploiting you, men and women who want you to be free, really and truly free. You dislike such men and women, because they are alien to your nature. They are simple and forthright; they value the truth as much as you value trickery. They see through you, not with contempt but with sorrow at the human condition; but your awareness of being seen through gives you a sense of danger. You recognize their greatness, little man, only when many other little men tell you they are great. You're afraid of great men, their closeness to life and love of life.

But the great man loves you as he would love any other animal, as a living creature. He doesn't want you to suffer as you've suffered for thousands of years. He doesn't want you to talk nonsense, as you've done for thousands of years. He doesn't want you to live like a work horse, because he loves life and wants it to be free from suffering and humiliation.

You drive truly great men to despise you, to hide their heads in sorrow at you and your smallness, to avoid you, and worst of all, to *pity* you. If, little man, you are a psychiatrist, a Lombroso for instance, you brand the truly great man a criminal, or at least a would-be criminal, or a lunatic, because a great man does not, like you, see the aim of life in riches, in socially suitable marriages for his daughters, or in a political career, or in academic honors. So, because he's different from yourself, you call him a "genius" or a "nut." He, for his part, is quite willing to admit that he's not a genius but only a living creature. You call him asocial because he'd rather be alone with his thoughts than listening to inane chatter at your social functions. You say he's crazy because he spends his money on scientific research instead of investing it in stocks as you do. You dare, little man, in your abysmal degeneracy, to call a simple, straightforward man "abnormal." You measure him against yourself and your petty standards of normalcy and find him wanting. You fail to see, little man, you refuse to recognize that you're driving this man, who loves you and wants only to help you, from all social life, because in drawing room and barroom alike, you've made it unbearable. Who made him what he is today after decades of desperate suffering? You did, with your unscrupulousness, your narrow-mindedness, your crooked

Inane chatter at your social functions

thinking, and your "eternal truths," which are incapable of surviving ten years of social development. Just think of all the "certainties" you've sworn by in the years between the First and Second World Wars alone. Tell me frankly, how much have you retracted? Nothing, little man. A great man is cautious in his thinking, but once he commits himself to an idea, he thinks far ahead. And you, little man, treat him like a pariah when his idea proves to be *sound* and long-lived, and yours a piddling flash in the pan. By making him into a pariah, you sow the terrible seed of loneliness in him. Not the seed that engenders great actions but the seed of fear, the fear of being misunderstood and abused by you. For you are "the people," "public opinion," "social con-science." Have you, little man, ever stopped to think of the enormous responsibility this implies? Have you ever asked yourself (tell the truth now!) whether, from the standpoint of long-term social development, or of nature, or of great human achievement—that of a Jesus, for example—your thinking is right or wrong? No, you never ask yourself whether your thinking is right or wrong. You ask yourself what your neighbor will say about it, or whether, if you do right, it will cost you money. That's what you ask yourself, little man; that and nothing else!

After driving the great man into solitude, you forgot what you did to him. You merely talked more nonsense, played another dirty trick, inflicted another deep hurt. You forget. But a great man doesn't forget. He doesn't plot revenge but TRIES TO UNDERSTAND WHY YOU BEHAVE SO MISERABLY. I know that too is beyond you. But believe me: even if you hurt him any number of times, even if you inflict wounds that can never heal, even if a moment after your petty misdeed you forget what you've done, the great man suffers for your misdeeds in your stead, not because they are great but because they are petty. He tries to understand what it is that makes you sling mud at the husband or wife who has disappointed you, torment a child because some vicious neighbor has taken a dislike to him, betray your friends, ridicule the kindly but get what you can out of them, and cringe under the whip. He tries to understand what makes you *take what is given, give what is demanded of you, but never give freely and lovingly;* what makes you kick those who are down or on the way down, lie instead of telling the truth, and persecute not lies but the truth. Little man, you're always on the side of the persecutors.

To win your favor, little man, to gain your worthless

friendship, a great man would have to adapt himself to your ways, to say what you want to hear, to preen himself with your virtues. But he would not be great and true and simple, he would not be a great man if he had your virtues, your language, and your friendship. You can't help seeing that your friends, who say what you want to hear, have never been great men.

You don't believe that *your* friend could ever do anything great. You despise yourself in secret, even—no, especially—when you stand on your dignity; and since you despise yourself, you are unable to respect your friend. You can't bring yourself to believe that anyone you have sat at table with, or shared a house with, is capable of great achievement. That is why all great men have been solitary. It is hard to think in your company, little man. One can only think *about* you or *for your benefit,* not *with* you, for you stifle all big, generous ideas. If you're a mother, you say to your thinking child, "It's not fit for children." If you're a professor of biology, you say, "No serious student can subscribe to that. What! Doubt the existence of germs in the air?!" If you're a teacher, you say, "A well-behaved child doesn't ask impertinent questions." And if you're a wife, you say, "A discovery? You've made a discovery? If I were you, I'd go to work and support my family!" But when the discovery comes out in the paper, little man, then you believe it whether you understand it or not.

I tell you, little man, you've lost all feeling for the best that is in you. You've stifled it. And when you find something worthwhile in others, in your children, your wife, your husband, your father or mother, you kill it. Little man, you're small and you want to stay small.

"Germs in the air"

But when the discovery comes out in the paper,
you believe it whether you understand it or not

How, you ask me, do I know all this? I'll tell you.

I have known you, shared your experiences; I've known you in myself. As a physician I've freed you from what is small in you; as an educator I've often guided you in the path of integrity and openness. I know how bitterly you resist your integrity, what mortal fear comes over you when called upon to follow your own, authentic nature.

You are not always small, little man. I know you have your "great moments," your "flights of enthusiasm" and "exaltation." But you lack the perseverance to let your enthusiasm soar, to let your exaltation carry you higher and higher. You're afraid to soar, afraid of heights and depths. Nietzsche told you that long ago, far better than I can. He wanted to raise you up to be a superman, to surpass the merely human. His superman became your Führer, Hitler. And you have remained what you were, the subhuman.

I want you to stop being subhuman and become "yourself." "Yourself," I say. Not the newspaper you read, not your vicious neighbor's opinion, but "yourself." I know, and you don't, what you really are deep down. Deep down, you are what a deer, your God, your poet, or your philosopher is. But you think you're a member of the VFW, your bowling club, or the Ku Klux Klan. And because you think so, you behave as you do. This too was told you long ago, by Heinrich Mann in Germany, by Upton Sinclair and John Dos Passos in the United States. But you recognized neither Mann nor Sinclair. You recognize only the heavy-weight champion and Al Capone. If given your choice between a library and a fight, you'll undoubtedly go to the fight.

You plead for happiness in life, but security means more to you, even if it costs you your backbone or wrecks your

You're afraid to soar, afraid of heights and depths

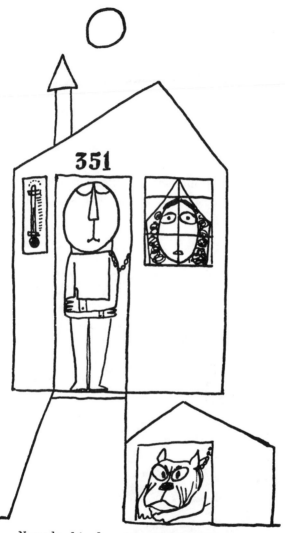

You plead for happiness in life, but security means more to you

whole life. Since you have never learned to seize upon happiness, to enjoy it and safeguard it, you lack the courage of integrity. Shall I tell you, little man, what kind of man you are? You listen to commercials on the radio, advertisements for laxatives, toothpaste, shoe polish, deodorants, and so on. But you are unaware of the abysmal stupidity, the abominable bad taste of the siren's tones calculated to catch *your* ear. Have you ever listened closely to a nightclub entertainer's jokes about you? About you, about himself, and your whole wretched world. Listen to your advertisements for better bowel movements and learn who and what you are.

Listen, little man! Every single one of your *petty* misdeeds throws a light on the wretchedness of human life. Every one of your petty actions diminishes the hope of improving your lot just a little more. That is ground for sorrow, little man, for deep, heartbreaking sorrow. To avert such sorrow you make silly little jokes. That's what you call your sense of humor.

You hear a joke about yourself and you join in the laughter. You don't laugh because you appreciate humor at your own expense. You laugh at the little man without suspecting that you are laughing at yourself, that *the joke is on you*. And all the millions of little men fail to realize that the joke is on them. Why have you been laughed at so heartily, so openly, so maliciously down through the centuries? Have you ever noticed how ridiculous the common people are made to look in the movies?

I will tell you why you are laughed at, little man, because *I take you seriously, very seriously*.

Invariably you miss the truth in your thinking. You remind me of the whimsical sharpshooter who purposely

You hear a joke about yourself and you
join in the laughter

misses the bull's eye by a hair's breadth. You disagree? I'll prove it.

You could have become the master of your existence long ago if your thinking aimed at the truth. I'll give you an example of your thinking:

"It's all the fault of the Jews," you say. "What's a Jew?" I ask. "People with Jewish blood," you say. "How do you distinguish Jewish blood from other blood?" The question baffles you. You hesitate. Then you say, "I meant the Jewish race." "What's race?" I ask. "Race? That's obvious. Just as there's a Germanic race, there's a Jewish race." "What are the characteristics of the Jewish race?" "A Jew has black hair, a long hooked nose, and sharp eyes. The Jews are greedy and capitalistic." "Have you ever seen a southern Frenchman or an Italian side by side with a Jew? Can you distinguish between them?" "No, not really . . ."

"Then what's a Jew? His blood picture is the same as everyone else's. His appearance is no different from that of a Frenchman or an Italian. On the other hand, have you ever seen any German Jews?" "They look like Germans." "What's a German?" "A German is a member of the Nordic Aryan race." "Are the Indians Aryans?" "Yes." "Are they Nordics?" "No." "Are they blond?" "No." "See? You don't even know what a Jew or a German is." "But Jews do exist!" "Of course Jews exist. So do Christians and Mohammedans." "That's right. I meant the Jewish religion." "Was Roosevelt a Dutchman?" "No." "Why do you call a descendant of David a Jew if you don't call Roosevelt a Dutchman?" "The Jews are different." "What's different?" "I don't know."

That's the kind of rubbish you talk, little man. And with such rubbish you set up armed gangs that kill ten million people for being Jews, though you can't even tell me what a Jew is. That's why you're laughed at, why anybody with anything serious to do steers clear of you. That's why you're up to your neck in muck. It makes you feel superior to call someone a Jew. It makes you feel superior because you feel inferior. You feel inferior because you yourself are exactly what you want to kill off in the people you call Jews. That's just a sampling of the truth about you, little man.

When you contemptuously call someone a "Jew," your sense of your own littleness is relieved. I discovered that only recently. You call anyone who arouses too much or too little respect in you a Jew. And as if you'd been sent down to earth by some higher power, you take it on yourself to decide who is a Jew. I contest that right, regardless of whether you're a little Aryan or a little Jew. No one but myself is entitled to say what I am. I am a biological and cultural mongrel and proud of it; in mind and body, I am a product of *all* classes and races and nations. I don't pretend to be racially or socially pure like you, or a chauvinist like you, petty fascist of all nations, races, and classes. I'm told that you didn't want a Jewish engineer in Palestine because he was uncircumcised. I have nothing more in common with Jewish fascists than with any other fascists. I am moved by no feeling for the Jewish language, Jewish religion, or Jewish culture. I believe in the Jewish God no more than in the Christian or Indian God, but I know where you get your God. I don't believe that the Jews are God's "chosen people." I believe that someday the Jewish people will lose themselves among the masses of human animals on this planet and that this will be a good thing for them and their descendants. You don't like to hear that, little Jewish man. You harp on your Jewishness because you despise yourself and those close to you *as Jews*. The Jew himself is the worst Jew hater of all. That's an old truth. But I don't despise you and I don't hate you. I simply have nothing in common with you, at any rate no more than with a Chinese or a raccoon, namely, our common origin in cosmic matter. Why do you stop at Shem, little Jew, why not go back to protoplasm? To my mind, life begins with plasmatic contraction, not with rabbinic theology.

It took many millions of years for you to evolve from a jellyfish to a terrestrial biped. You have been living in bodily rigidity, your present aberration, for only six thousand years. It will take you a hundred or five hundred or five thousand years to rediscover the nature in yourself, the jellyfish in you.

*It took many millions of years for you to evolve
from a jellyfish to a terrestrial biped*

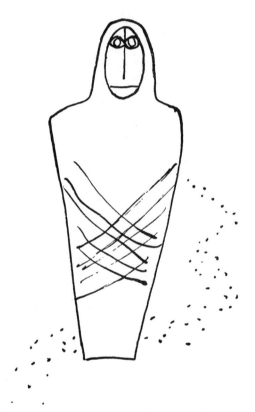

You have lived in bodily rigidity, your present aberration, for only six thousand years

I have discovered the jellyfish in you and have described it to you clearly. The first time you heard of it, you proclaimed me a new genius. You remember, no doubt; it was in Scandinavia, when you were casting about for a new Lenin. I had other things to do and declined the honor. You also proclaimed me a new Darwin, Marx, Pasteur, and Freud. Even then I told you that you'd be able to speak and write as well as I do if only, oh, you chosen little man, you'd stop shouting hurrah, hurrah. Because these cries of victory becloud your reason and stultify your creative nature.

Is it not true, little man, that you persecute "unwed mothers" as immoral? Is it not true that you draw a sharp distinction between "legitimate" and "illegitimate" children? What a pitiful creature you are to be running around loose in this vale of tears! You don't know the meaning of your own words.

You worship the Christ child. The Christ child was born of a mother who had no marriage certificate. What you worship in the Christ child, you poor little marriage-ridden man, is your own yearning for sexual freedom! You exalted the "illegitimate" Christ child, made him into the son of God, who regarded no child as illegitimate. But then, cruel and small as you are, you began, in the person of the Apostle Paul, to persecute the children of true love and to give the children of true hate the protection of your religious laws. You are a *vile* little man.

You drive your cars across bridges conceived by the great Galileo. Do you know, little man of all countries, that the great Galileo begot three children without a marriage certificate? You don't tell your schoolchildren that.

And wasn't that one of your reasons for persecuting Galileo?

And little man in the fatherland of all the Slavic peoples, do you know that when he came to power, the great Lenin, father of all the workers of the world (or of all the Slavs?), abolished your compulsory marriage? Do you know that he himself had lived with a woman out of wedlock? Of this you made a secret, didn't you, little man? And then, through your great leader of all the Slavs, you revived the old marriage laws because you were incapable of embodying Lenin's great deed in your lives?

Of all that you know nothing. What are truth, history, and the struggle for your freedom to you? And who are you, anyway, to have an opinion of your own?

You don't so much as suspect that it's your own prurient imagination and your sexual irresponsibility that have made you fetter yourself with such marriage laws.

I've said it before and I say it again: you feel wretched and small, and stinking and mentally mutilated; you feel impotent, tense, rigid, lifeless, and empty. You haven't got a girl; or if you have, your only thought is to fuck her to prove you're a man. You don't know the meaning of love. You're constipated. You take laxatives. You smell bad, your skin is clammy or leathery. You have no feeling for the child in your arms, so you want to turn him into a little whipped dog.

All your life you've been tormented by your impotence. It creeps into all your thoughts. It interferes with your work. Your wife has left you because you couldn't give her love. You suffer from compulsions, cardiac anxiety, and nervous tensions. You can't stop thinking about sex. Somebody tells you about my sex-economy, tells you that I understand you and want to help you. I want to enable you to have your sexual life at night, so you can work in the daytime, free from thoughts about sex. I want your wife to be happy in your arms and not desperate. I want your children to be rosy-cheeked and not pale, loving and not cruel. But you say, "Sex isn't the only thing in life. There are other, more important things." That's the way you are, little man.

Or maybe, little man, you're a Marxist, a "professional revolutionary," a future leader of the workers of the world, a future father of some Soviet fatherland. You want to free the world from its sufferings. The misguided workers run away from you and you run after them, shouting, "Stop, stop, ye toiling masses! Can't you see that I'm your liberator? Why won't you admit it? Down with capitalism!" I put life into your masses, little revolutionary; I show them the wretchedness of their petty lives. They listen to me, they glow with hope and enthusiasm and run to your organizations because they expect to find *me* there. And what do *you* do? "Sex is a petit-bourgeois aberration," you say. "Everything depends on economic factors." And you read Van de Velde's book about love techniques.

When a great man set to work building a scientific foundation for your emancipation, you let him starve. You crushed the first campaign of truth against your deviation from the laws of life. When his campaign nevertheless proved successful, in spite of you, you took over its management and crushed it a second time. The first time the great man dissolved your organization. The second time he was unable to oppose you, because he was dead. You didn't understand that in labor, *your* labor, he had found the vital force that creates value. You didn't understand that his theory of society was designed to protect your "society" against the "state." *You understood nothing at all!*

And even with your "economic factors" you don't accomplish anything. A great and wise man worked all his life trying to teach you that you have to improve the economy if you want to get something out of life; that a civilization cannot be built by starving people but requires the development of *every* sphere of life; that you must free your society from *all* tyranny. That truly great man made only two mistakes in his efforts to enlighten you. He believed that you were capable of freedom and capable of safeguarding your freedom once you had won it. And his second mistake was to proclaim you, the proletarian, a dictator.

And you, little man, what did you do with the great man's intellectual wealth? He gave you lofty, far-reaching ideas, but you retained only one resounding word: dictatorship! Of all the superabundance of a great warm heart . . . only one word remained: dictatorship! You threw everything else overboard—freedom, respect for the truth, liberation from economic slavery, methodical, constructive thinking. Only one ill-chosen, though well-meant word stayed with you: *dictatorship!*

From this little blunder on the part of a wise man you built up an enormous system of lies, persecution, torture, prisons, executioners, secret police, informers, and stool pigeons, uniforms, marshals, and medals. Everything else you threw overboard. Now are you beginning to understand what you are like, little man? Not yet? All right, let's try again: you confused the "economic conditions" of your welfare in life and love with "machinery"; the

Uniforms, marshals, and medals

emancipation of man with the "greatness of the state"; willingness to make sacrifices for great purposes with stupid, pigheaded "party discipline"; the awakening of the millions with the parading of armed might; liberated love with indiscriminate rape when you came to Germany; the abolition of poverty with the extermination of the poor, weak, and helpless; child care with the "breeding of patriots"; family planning with medals for the "mothers of ten children." Haven't you yourself been victimized by this "mother of ten children" idea of yours?

The "Workers' Fatherland" isn't the only country where that ill-omened word "dictatorship" resounded in your ears. Elsewhere you dressed it in resplendent uniforms and from your ranks engendered the impotent, mystical, sadistic house painter who led you to the Third Reich and sixty million of your kind to the grave. And you went right on shouting: Hurrah! Hurrah! Hurrah!

That's the way you are, little man. But nobody dares to tell you. Because they're afraid of you; they want you to be little.

You consume your happiness.

You have never enjoyed happiness in full freedom, little man. That's why you consume it, why you take no responsibility for the preservation of your happiness. You haven't learned (you never had a chance) to cultivate your happiness with loving care, as a gardener cultivates his flowers and a farmer his wheat. Great scientists and poets and philosophers have kept away from you, little man, because in your company it is easy to consume happiness but hard to cultivate it, and they were eager to cultivate theirs.

You consume your happiness

You don't catch my meaning, little man? All right, I'll explain.

A discoverer works hard for ten, twenty, thirty years on his science, his machine, or his social idea. Its newness is a staggering burden and he has to bear it all by himself. Over the years he suffers from your stupidities, your puny, false ideas and ideals, learns to analyze and understand them, and finally replaces them by new ideas. Little man, you don't help him in his work. Far from it! You don't go to him and say, "My friend, I see how hard you're working. I also see that you're working on *my* machine, or working for *my* child, *my* wife, *my* friend, *my* house, *my* field. I have long been plagued with troubles but unable to help myself. Can I help you to help me?" No, little man, you never go to your helper to help him. You shout hurrah, hurrah, or you play cards, or you bellow at a fight, or you slave away in a factory or mine. But you never offer to help your helper. And I'll tell you why. Because at the beginning of his labor the discoverer has nothing to offer but *ideas*. No profits, no pay increase, no union wage scale, no Christmas bonus, and none of the comforts of life. All he has to share are troubles, and you want no troubles; maybe you already have more of them than you need.

But if you merely kept away and refrained from helping him, the discoverer wouldn't be unhappy on your account. He doesn't think and worry and discover "for" you. He does all this because he is driven by his own functional aliveness. He leaves it to the party leaders and clergymen to minister to you and take care of you and pity you. He thinks it's high time you learned to *take care of yourself*.

But you don't content yourself with not helping; you

harass him and spit at him. When after years of hard work the discoverer finally comes to understand why you are incapable of giving your wife happiness in love, you go and tell him *he* is sexually debased. You say that because *you* are sexually debased and *therefore* incapable of love, but that never dawns on you. If the discoverer has just found out why people are dying like flies of cancer, and you, little man, happen to be a professor of cancer pathology with a well-paid job at a cancer hospital, you say he's a fake, or that he knows nothing about air germs, or that he has spent or been given too much money for his research, or you ask him if he's a Jew or a foreigner, or you insist on examining him to determine whether he is qualified to deal with "your" cancer, and you prefer to let many, many cancer patients die rather than admit that *he* has discovered what would enable *you* to save your patients. Your academic standing or your pocketbook or your connections with the radium industry mean more to you than truth and knowledge. Little man, you are and remain small and vile.

I repeat: not only do you not help but you interfere maliciously with the work the discoverer does *for you* or instead of you. Now do you understand why happiness runs away from you? *Happiness wants to be worked for and earned.* But you merely want to consume happiness. It runs away because it doesn't want to be consumed by you.

In the meantime, the discoverer has managed to convince a good many people that his discovery has practical value, that it offers a possibility of understanding certain psychic disorders, or of lifting a weight, or blasting rock, or healing tumors, or seeing through opaque matter with the help of rays. You don't believe it until you see it in the paper, because you don't trust your own eyes and intelligence. When the discovery appears in the papers, you come running. Suddenly the discoverer, whom only a short while before you were denigrating as a charlatan, pornographer, faker, and menace to public morality, becomes a "genius." You don't know what a genius is, little man. Any more than you know what a "Jew" or "truth" or "happiness" is. Let me tell you what Jack London said about genius in his *Martin Eden*. I'm sure millions of you have read it, but you haven't understood. *"Genius" is the trade mark you paste on your products when you put them up for sale.* If the discoverer (who only a little while ago was a "sex fiend" or a "psychotic") turns out to be a "genius," you will be in more of a hurry to *consume* the happiness he has brought into the world. In fact, you'll gobble it up, because *millions* of little men will come out and shout "Genius, genius" in chorus with you. People will come in droves and eat your products out of your hand. If you're a doctor, patients will flock to you. You will be able to help them more quickly and more effectively, and you will make much more money than before. "What's wrong with that?" I hear you say, little man. Nothing's wrong with it, of course not. There's nothing wrong with making money by good honest work. But *it is wrong* not to give anything back to the discovery, not to cultivate it but only to exploit it, *only* to get rich from it. And that's exactly what you do. You do nothing to develop the great discovery in the right direction. You take it over mechanically, heedlessly, greedily, stupidly. You fail to see its possibilities or its limits. You are too short on feeling for life to see the possibilities, and at the same time you overstep the limits. If as a physician or bacteriologist you know typhoid and cholera to be infectious diseases, you will be sure to waste thirty years of research by looking for a cancer bacillus. Having learned from a great man that machines operate in accordance with certain laws, you build machines for the purpose of killing and regard living things as machines. In this you have gone astray, not for three decades but for three centuries. You have imprinted false conceptions indelibly on the minds of many thousands of scientific workers, and moreover done direct and serious injury to life itself, because, on the basis of this fallacy, you have been led, for the sake of your dignity or your professorship or your religion or your pocketbook or your character armor, to persecute, slander, imprison, or otherwise damage anyone who was really on the track of the life function.

I know, I know, you want your "geniuses" and you're ready to honor them. But you want *nice* geniuses, well-behaved, moderate geniuses with no nonsense about them, and not the untamed variety who break through all barriers and limitations. You want a limited, cropped and clipped genius you can parade through the streets of your cities without embarrassment.

That's the way you are, little man. You can spoon it in to the last drop, you can help yourself and gobble it up, but *you can't create*. And that's why you're where you are and what you are; why you spend your whole life in a dismal office, punching an adding machine or hunched over a drawing board, or in the straitjacket of marriage, or in a schoolroom teaching, though you hate children. You're incapable of developing, you'll never get a new idea, be-

45

You want nice, cropped and clipped geniuses
you can parade through the streets of your cities
without embarrassment

cause you've always taken freely but given nothing, because you've always helped yourself to what someone else has given you ready-made.

You don't understand why this is so and must be so? I can tell you, little man, because when you came to me with your inner emptiness or your impotence or your psychic disorder, I learned to recognize you as a rigid animal. You can only gobble and take, you're incapable of creating or giving, because your basic bodily attitude is one of *holding back* and of defiant mistrust; because you panic when the primordial impulse to love and to give

46

stirs in you. That's why you're *afraid of giving*. And essentially your way of taking means only one thing: you have to stuff yourself full of money, food, happiness, and knowledge, because you feel empty, starved, and unhappy, devoid both of true knowledge and the desire for knowledge. That's why you go to such lengths to sidestep the truth, little man. The truth might arouse a love reflex. It might, in fact it would, show you what I'm trying, if only inadequately, to show you now. And that, little man, you don't want. You want only to be a consumer and a patriot.

"Did you hear that? He's attacking patriotism, the mainstay of the state and of its germ cell, the family. This must be stopped!"

That's the way you yell, little man, when someone calls your attention to your psychic constipation. You don't want to know, you don't want to listen. You want to shout hurrah. I let you shout hurrah, but you won't let me tell you why you're incapable of happiness. I see fear in your eyes, because my question hits you deep down. You're in favor of "religious tolerance." You demand freedom to love your religion, whatever it may be. So far so good. But you want more than that: you want everybody to observe *your* religion. You're tolerant toward your religion but no other. And it sends you into a rage that anyone should worship not a personal God but nature, that he should love nature and try to understand it. When a married couple find they can no longer live together, you want one member to hale the other into court with accusations of immorality or brutality. And, oh, you puny descendant of great rebels, you refuse to countenance divorce by common consent. You're afraid of your own prurience.

47

You want the truth in a mirror, where you can't take hold of it and it can't take hold of you. Your chauvinism, little man, springs from your bodily rigidity, from your mental constipation. I don't say this to scoff at you, I say it because I'm your friend, even if you tend to kill your friends when they tell you the truth. Take a look at your patriots: they don't walk, they march. They don't hate their true enemy; they have hereditary enemies, who change every ten years, from sworn enemy to lifelong friend and back again to sworn enemy. They don't sing songs, they bellow anthems. They don't embrace their girls; they fuck them and tot up their score for the night. The worst you can do is kill me, just as you've liquidated so many of your true friends: Jesus, Rathenau, the warmhearted Karl Lieb-knecht, Lincoln, and many more. But patriotism has liquidated *you*, little man, trampled and crushed you by the millions. And still you're determined to go on being a patriot.

You yearn for love; you love your work and live on it, and your work lives on my knowledge and that of others. Love, work, and knowledge know no fatherlands, no customs barriers, no uniforms. But you want to be a little patriot, because you're afraid of true love, afraid of taking responsibility for your own work, and mortally afraid of knowledge. That is why you can only spoon up the love, work, and knowledge of others and can never *create*. That is why you steal your happiness like a thief in the night, why the sight of true happiness turns you green with envy.

"Stop thief! He's a foreigner, an immigrant. Whereas I'm a German, an American, a Dane, a Norwegian!"

That's why you steal your happiness
like a thief in the night

Stop foaming at the mouth, little man! You are and always will be an immigrant and an emigrant. You immigrated into this world by pure accident and will emigrate from it without fanfare. You screech because you're afraid, mortally afraid. You feel that your body is growing rigid and gradually drying up. That's why you're afraid, why you call for your police. But even your police have no power over the truth. Even your policeman comes to me with his troubles: his wife's in bad shape, his children are sick. His uniform and revolver hide what's human in him. But he can't hide it from me; I've seen your policeman naked.

"Is he registered with the police? Are his papers in order? Has he paid his taxes? Investigate him. The honor and security of the nation are at stake."

Yes, little man, I've always been properly registered,

You screech because you're afraid

I've always paid my taxes. It's not the honor and security of the nation that you're worried about. You're scared to death that I might show you to the world as I've seen you in my consultation room. That's why you're trying so hard to have me jailed for sedition. I know you, little man! If you happen to be a district attorney, your aim in life is not to *uphold* justice; no, what you're after is a sensational case that will get you a promotion. That's what all little district attorneys are after. Your treatment of Socrates was a case in point. But you never learn from history. You murdered Socrates, and that's why you're still in the muck. That's right: you murdered Socrates and to this day you don't know it. You accused him of undermining your morality. He's still undermining it, you poor little man. You murdered his body but not his spirit. And you're still committing murder in the name of law and order, but you do it in a cowardly, underhanded way. You don't dare look me in the eye when you accuse me of immorality, because you know which of us two is immoral, prurient, and obscene. Somebody once said that among all his many friends he could think of only one who had never told a dirty joke; he was referring to me. Little man, whether you're a district attorney, a judge, or a chief of police, I know your dirty jokes. And I know where they come from. So I'd advise you to keep quiet. In a pinch you might succeed in proving that my last tax payment was a hundred dollars too short, or that I've crossed a state line with a woman, or that I've spoken kindly to a child. It's on *your* lips, not mine, that such statements come to sound ugly and obscene, because of what your low pettifogging mind reads into them. And because you can't behave in any other way, you think I'm like you. No, my little man, I'm not like you in these things, and never was. It makes no difference whether you believe me or not. To be sure, you have a revolver and I have knowledge. Each man to his trade.

Let me tell you, little man, how you ruin your own life.

In 1924 I proposed a scientific study of the human character. You were enthusiastic.

In 1928 our work began to show results. You called me an "outstanding thinker."

In 1933 your publishing house was on the point of bringing out my findings in book form. Hitler had just come to power; I was teaching you to understand that Hitler became powerful because your character is armored.

You refused to publish the book,* in which I showed you how you and no one else had produced Hitler.

Nevertheless my book appeared and you were enthusiastic. But you killed it with silence because your "president" had banned it. He had also advised mothers to repress the genital excitations of infants by having them hold their breath.

For twelve years you were silent about my book despite your enthusiasm.

In 1945 it was republished. You hailed it as a "classic." You are still enthusiastic about it.

Twenty-two years, twenty-two long, eventful, anguished years have passed since I began to teach you that what matters is not individual therapy but the prevention of psychic disorders. And again you're behaving as you've behaved for thousands of years. For twenty-two long fearful years I taught you that people succumb to madness of one kind or another or live in misery of one kind or another because they have become rigid in body and soul and because they are capable neither of enjoying love nor of giving it, because their bodies cannot, like those of all other animals, convulse in the act of love.

Twenty-two years after I first told you so, you tell your friends that the essential is not the cure but the prevention of psychic disorders. But you go on behaving as you've behaved for thousands of years. You state the great aim, without mentioning how it's to be attained. *You don't mention the love life of the masses.* You want "to prevent psychic disorders"—that much it's permissible to say—

* *Character Analysis*—Ed.

without going into the disaster of people's sexual lives—
that is forbidden. As a physician, you're still up to your
neck in the swamp.

What would you think of an engineer who expounded
the art of flying without revealing the secrets of the engine
and propeller? That's what you do, you engineer of the
human soul. Just that. You're a coward. You want the
raisins out of my cake but you don't want the thorns
of my roses. Haven't you too, little psychiatrist, been
cracking silly jokes about me? Haven't you ridiculed me
as "the prophet of bigger and better orgasms"? Have you
never heard the whimpering of a young wife whose body
has been desecrated by an impotent husband? Or the
anguished cry of an adolescent bursting with unfulfilled
love? Does your security still mean more to you than your
patient? How long will you go on valuing your respect-
ability above your medical mission? How long will you
refuse to see that your pussyfooting procrastination is
costing millions their lives?

You put security before truth.

When you hear about my orgone, you don't ask, "What
can it do to cure the sick?" No. You ask, "Is he licensed
to practice medicine in the state of Maine?" Don't you
realize that though you and your wretched licenses can
obstruct my work a little, you can't stop it; that I have
a worldwide reputation as the discoverer of your emotional
plague and the investigator of your life energy; that no
one is entitled to examine me unless he knows more than
I do?

You fritter away your freedom. No one has ever asked
you, little man, why you haven't been more successful in

winning freedom, or if you have won it, why you have quickly lost it to a new master.

"Did you hear that? He has the gall to cast doubt on democracy and the revolutionary upsurge of the workers of the world. Down with the revolutionary, down with the counter-revolutionary! Down!"

Take it easy, little Führer of all democrats and of the world proletariat. I am convinced that your *real* prospects of attaining freedom depend more on the answer to that one question than on ten thousand resolutions of your party congresses.

"Down with him! He has insulted the nation and the vanguard of the revolutionary proletariat! Down with him! Stand him up against the wall!"

All your cries of "Up" and "Down" won't bring you one

Down with him!

step closer to your goal, little man. You have always thought you could safeguard your freedom by standing people "up against the wall." *You'd do better to stand yourself up to a mirror . . .*

"Down! . . ."

Take it easy, little man. I don't mean to insult you, I'm only trying to show you why you've never been able to win freedom, or to preserve it for any length of time. Doesn't that interest you at all?

"Do—o—own . . ."

All right. I'll be brief. Let me tell you how the little man in you behaves when you find yourself in a situation of freedom. Suppose you're a student at an institute dedicated to the sexual health of children and adolescents. You're enthusiastic about the "brilliant idea," you want to participate in the liberation movement. The following happened in my institute:

My students were bending over their microscopes, observing earth bions. You were sitting naked in the orgone accumulator. I called to you, asking you to come and take a look. Whereupon you came bouncing out of the accumulator stark naked, exposing your nudity to the women and young girls. I reprimanded you, but you didn't understand. And I failed to understand why *you* didn't understand. Later, when we talked it over at length, you admitted that this had been your idea of the freedom you would find at an institute dedicated to the sexual health of children and of all mankind. With my help you soon found out that you had behaved indecently because you *despised* the institute and its underlying idea. Have I made myself clear? . . . Nothing to say? Then I'll go on.

Another example of how you fritter away your freedom:

You know and I know, everybody knows, that you're perpetually sex-starved, that you mentally feel up every member of the opposite sex who comes your way, that you and your friends are constantly telling dirty stories about sex; in short, that you have a sordid, *pornographic* imagination. One night I heard you marching through the streets, howling in chorus, "We want women! We want women!"

Worried about you, I organized clubs, where I hoped you would learn to understand the wretchedness of your life and to surmount it. You and your friends flocked to these clubs. Why, little man? I thought it was because of a sincere interest in improving your lives. I was slow to discover the real reason. You regarded the clubs as a new kind of brothel where girls could be had free of charge. When that became clear to me, I disbanded the clubs. Not because I thought it was wrong to meet a girl at a club but because you behaved like a rutting pig. So the clubs were discontinued and once again you remained in the muck . . . You wish to say something?

"The proletariat has been corrupted by the bourgeoisie. The leaders of the world proletariat will know what to do. They'll clean up the stable with an iron hand. And anyway, the sexual problem of the proletariat will solve itself!"

I know exactly what you mean, little man. In the Workers' Fatherland they let the sexual problem solve itself. The results could be seen in Berlin when, night after night, the proletarian soldiers raped every woman they could lay hands on. Be still! You know it's true. Your champions of "revolutionary honor," your "soldiers of proletarian freedom" have disgraced you for centuries to come . . . You say that could "only have happened in war"? All right, I'll tell you another true story.

A coming leader, who hadn't yet made it, was as enthusiastic about sex-economy as he was about the dictatorship of the proletariat. He came to me and said, "You're wonderful. Karl Marx taught people how to be *economically* free. And you taught them how to be *sexually* free. You said to them, 'Go forth and fuck.'" Your mind perverts every idea. In your life my loving embrace becomes an act of pornography.

You don't know what I'm talking about, little man. That's why you keep sinking back into the swamp.

Little woman, if without any particular vocation you drifted into teaching merely because you had no children of your own, you're doing unconscionable harm. You're supposed to be bringing up children. The rearing of children, if taken seriously, implies the correct handling of their sexuality. *In order to handle a child's sexuality correctly, one must know from one's own experience what love is.* But you're built like a tub, you're awkward and physically repulsive. That alone is enough to give you a bitter, deep-seated hatred for every attractive, living body. Naturally I don't blame you for being built like a tub, or for never having experienced love (no healthy man could have loved you), or for failing to understand love in children. But I do blame you for making a virtue of your affliction, of your wrecked, tublike body, of your lack of beauty and grace and your incapacity for love, and for stifling love in children. That, you ugly little woman, is a crime. Your existence is harmful because you turn healthy children against their healthy fathers, because you treat healthy childlike love as a symptom of disease, because, ugly little woman, not content with looking like a tub, you think and teach like a tub; because instead of withdrawing modestly into a quiet corner of life, you do your best to imprint all life with your ugliness, your tublike ungainliness, your hypocrisy, and with the bitter hatred that you hide behind your phony smile.

And you, little man, leave your healthy children to the mercies of such women, who inject bitterness and venom into their healthy souls. And that is why you are as you are, why you live as you live and think as you think. That is why the world is as it is.

This is what you're like, little man. You came to me to learn what I had learned by hard work and struggle. If not for me, you'd be a small, unknown medical practitioner in some small town. I raised you up, I gave you knowledge and my therapeutic skill. I taught you to see how day by day and hour by hour freedom dies out and servitude is fostered. You were given a responsible position as my representative in a distant country. You were free in every sense of the word. I had confidence in your integrity. But you felt inwardly dependent on me because you hadn't been able to make very much of yourself. You needed me, because from me you drew knowledge, self-confidence, vision, and above all *development*. All this I gave you gladly, little man. I asked nothing in return. But then you start saying that I've raped you. You get insolent, imagining that that will make you "free." But mistaking insolence for freedom has always been the hallmark of the slave. Invoking your freedom, you refuse to send reports on your work.

*Not content with looking like a tub, you think
and teach like a tub; you do your best
to imprint all life with your
ugliness, your tublike ungainliness,
your hypocrisy, and with the bitter hatred
that you hide behind your phony smile*

And now you feel free . . . free from cooperation and responsibility. That, little man, is why you and the world are where you are.

Have you ever stopped to think, little man, how it feels to be an eagle with a nestful of hen's eggs? The eagle expects them to hatch out into little eagles, which he will raise to be big eagles. But one by one the shells crack and nothing comes out but little chicks. In his despair the eagle clings to the hope that the chicks will turn into eagles. But they all grow up to be cackling chickens. When this becomes clear to the eagle, his first impulse is to devour all the chicks and cackling chickens. The one thing that deters him from this wise crime is the forlorn hope that someday one of all these little chicks may turn out to be a little eagle, who will grow up to be a big eagle, able like himself to look far into the distance from his lofty crag and discover new worlds, new ideas, new ways of life. Only this one forlorn hope deters the lonely, sorrowful eagle from devouring all the cackling chicks and chickens. For they don't know that an eagle hatched them. They don't know they are living on a steep, lofty crag, high above the damp dark valleys. They don't look into the distance like the lonely eagle. All they do is eat and eat and eat what the eagle brings home for them. They creep under his powerful wings for warmth when the storm rages, and he stands up to it unaided. Or when things get too bad, they run away and throw sharp little stones at him from their hiding places, deliberately trying to hurt him. Under the first impact of their treachery, he is about to devour them. But he thinks it over and feels sorry for them. Someday, he thinks and hopes, someday a little eagle will surely turn up among all the cackling, gobbling, shortsighted chickens, a little eagle who will grow up to be like himself.

To this day, the lonely eagle has not given up his great hope. He is still hatching out little chicks . . .

You don't want to be an eagle, little man, and that's why the vultures devour you. You're afraid of eagles; that's why you live in herds and are devoured in herds. Because some of your hens have hatched out vulture eggs. And the vultures have become your leaders in your fight against the eagles, who wanted to lead you to faraway, better worlds. The vultures taught you to eat carrion, to content yourselves with a few crumbs of grain, and to shout, "Heil, great vulture!"

And now you're starving and dying in great herds, and you're still afraid of the eagles who hatch out your chicks.

Little man, you've built your house, your life, your culture, your civilization, your science and technology, your love and your methods of child-rearing, on sand. You don't know this, you don't want to know it, and when a great man tells you, you kill him. In your affliction you come and ask questions, always the same ones:

"My child is spiteful and cruel, constipated and pale; he smashes everything he can lay his hands on and screams with terror at night; he is backward at school. What should I do? Help me!"

Or: "My wife is frigid, she gives me no love. She tortures me, has fits of hysterical screaming, and runs around with a dozen other men. What should I do? Advise me!"

Or: "We won the last war, the war to end all wars. And now an even more horrible war has broken out. Help! What should I do?"

Or: "The civilization I was so proud of is collapsing

63

under the weight of inflation. Millions of people are starving, murdering, stealing, and going to the dogs. They have given up hope. Help! Tell me what to do!"

"What should I do? What should we do?" That has been your eternal question down through the ages.

It is the fate of great achievements, born from a way of life that sets truth before security, to be gobbled up by you and excreted in the form of shit.

For centuries great, brave, lonely men have been telling you what to do. Time and again you have corrupted, diminished, and demolished their teachings; time and again you have been captivated by their weakest points, taken not the great truth but some trifling error as your guiding principle. This, little man, is what you have done with Christianity, with the doctrine of the sovereign people, with socialism, with everything you touch. Why, you ask, do you do this? I don't believe you really want an answer. When you hear the truth, you'll cry bloody murder, or commit it.

You've done all this and built your house on sand because you're afraid or unable to feel the life-force within you, because you stifle and kill the love in your child before the child is even born; because you can't endure any free, living, natural movement or expression. It scares you out of your wits and you ask, "What will Mr. Jones say?"

You're afraid to think, little man, because thought goes hand in hand with intense bodily sensations and you're afraid of your body. Many great men have called out to you: Return to your origins! Hearken to your inner voice, respond to your true feelings. Hold love in honor and esteem! But you're deaf, you've lost all feeling for such

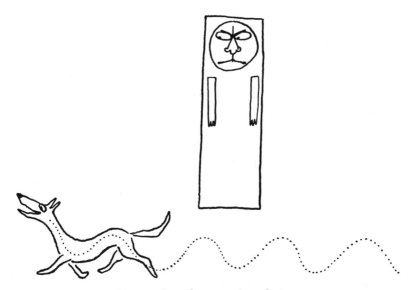

You can't endure any free, living,
natural movement or expression

words. They fall on vast deserts, little man, and the lonely heralds perish in your bleak wilderness.

You had your choice between soaring to superhuman heights with Nietzsche and sinking into subhuman depths with Hitler. You shouted Heil! Heil! and chose the subhuman.

You had your choice between Lenin's truly democratic constitution and Stalin's dictatorship. You chose Stalin's dictatorship.

You had your choice between Freud's elucidation of the sexual core of your psychic disorders and his theory of cultural adaptation. You dropped the theory of sexuality and chose his theory of cultural adaptation, which left you hanging in mid-air.

You had your choice between Jesus with his majestic simplicity and Paul with his celibacy for priests and life-long compulsory marriage for yourself. You chose the celibacy and compulsory marriage, and forgot the simplicity of Jesus's mother, who bore her child for love and love alone.

You had your choice between Marx's insight into the productivity of your living labor power, which alone creates the value of commodities, and the idea of the state. You forgot the living energy of your labor and chose the idea of the state.

In the French Revolution you had your choice between the cruel Robespierre and the great Danton. You chose cruelty and sent greatness and goodness to the guillotine.

In Germany you had your choice between Göring and Himmler on the one hand and Liebknecht, Landau, and Mühsam on the other. You made Himmler your police chief and murdered your great friends.

You had your choice between Julius Streicher and Walther Rathenau. You murdered Rathenau.

You had your choice between Lodge and Wilson. You murdered Wilson.

You had your choice between the cruel Inquisition and Galileo's truth. You tortured and humiliated the great Galileo, from whose inventions you are still benefiting, and now, in the twentieth century, you have brought the methods of the Inquisition to a new flowering.

You had your choice between shock therapy and the understanding of psychic disorder. You chose shock therapy for fear of seeing the enormity of your own wretchedness. You wanted to go on being blind where only wide-open, sharp-sighted eyes can help.

Only very recently you had your choice between murderous atomic energy and helpful orgone energy. Consistent in your wrong-headedness, you chose atomic energy.

You now have your choice between ignorance of the cancer cell and my disclosure of its secret, which can and will save millions of human lives. For years you've been repeating the same inanities in the press, but you haven't a word to say about the insight that might save your child, your wife, or your mother.

You are starving by the millions, little man of India, but you war with the Mohammedans over sacred cows. You go in rags, little Italian or Slav of Trieste, but the center of your preoccupations is whether Trieste should be Italian or Yugoslav. I always thought Trieste was a seaport for ships from all over the world!

You hang Nazis *after* they have killed millions of people. Where were you and what were you thinking about *before* those millions were killed? Mightn't a few hundred corpses have given you food for thought? Do you have to see millions of them before the humanity in you stirs?

Every one of your acts of smallness and meanness throws light on the boundless wretchedness of the human animal. "Why so tragic?" you ask. "Do you feel responsible for all evil?"

With remarks like that you condemn yourself. If, little man among millions, you were to shoulder the barest fraction of your responsibility, the world would be a very different place. Your great friends wouldn't perish, struck down by your smallness.

That's why your house still rests on sand. The roof is caving in on you, but you have your "proletarian" or "national" honor. The floor is sinking under your feet, and you sink with it, shouting, "Heil, my great Führer, long live the German, Russian, Jewish nation!" Your water pipes have burst and your child is drowning; but you still stand for "order and discipline" and try to whip them into your child. The wind is howling through your walls, your wife is in bed with pneumonia, but you, little man, continue to regard what would be a solid foundation for your existence as a figment of the "Jewish mind."

You come running to me and ask: "Dear, good, great Doctor! What should I do? What should we do? My whole house is collapsing, the wind is whistling through the cracks in the walls, my child is sick and my wife is miserable. I'm sick myself. What should I do? What should we do?"

"Build your house on granite. By granite I mean your nature that you're torturing to death, the love in your child's body, your wife's dream of love, your own dream of life when you were sixteen. Exchange your illusions for a bit of truth. Throw out your politicians and diplomats! Take your destiny into your own hands and build your life on rock. Forget about your neighbor and look inside yourself! Your neighbor, too, will be grateful. Tell your fellow workers all over the world that you're no longer willing to work for death but only for *life*. Instead of flocking to executions and shouting hurrah, hurrah, *make a law for the protection of human life and its blessings*. Such a law will be a part of the granite foundation your house rests on. Protect your small children's love against the assaults of lascivious, frustrated men and women. Stop the mouth

Throw out your politicians and diplomats

of the malignant old maid; expose her publicly or send her
to a reform school instead of young people who are longing
for love. Don't try to outdo your exploiter in exploitation
if you have a chance to become a boss. Throw away your
swallowtails and top hat, and stop applying for a license
to embrace your woman. Join forces with your kind in all
countries; they are like you, for better or worse. Let your
child grow up as nature (or 'God') intended. Don't try
to improve on nature. Learn to understand it and protect
it. Go to the library instead of the prize fight, go to foreign

69

countries rather than to Coney Island. And first and foremost, *think straight,* trust the quiet inner voice that tells you what to do. You hold your life in your hands, don't entrust it to anyone else, least of all to your chosen leaders. BE YOURSELF! Any number of great men have told you that."

"Would you listen to the reactionary petit-bourgeois individualist! Doesn't he know that history has its irreversible course and its dustbin, which is where he'll end up! 'Know yourself,' he says. Bourgeois rubbish! The revolutionary proletariat of all countries—led by its beloved leader, the father of all peoples, all Russians, Prussians and Pan-Slavs—will liberate the people! Down with all individualists and anarchists!"

Long live the fathers of all peoples and Slavs! Hurrah . . . hurrah! Listen to me, little man, I see trouble in store for you.

You're in the process of taking over; you know it and tremble at the thought. For centuries you'll murder your friends and hail the führers of all nations, of all proletarians, Russians and Prussians. Year in, year out, you'll hail one master after another. You won't hear the whimpering of your infants, the moans of your adolescents, the stifled longings of your wives or husbands, or, if you do, you'll dispose of all that as bourgeois individualism. On through the centuries you'll shed blood instead of safeguarding life, confident that with the executioner's help you're building your freedom. And day after day, year after year, you'll find yourself up to your ears in muck. On through the centuries you'll flock to hear Bigmouth, you'll cherish his words and succumb to his evil lures, but you'll be blind and deaf to the call of your own life. Because you're afraid of life, little man, mortally afraid. You do your best

Coney Island

You're afraid of life

to murder it, in the belief that you're building "socialism" or the "state" or "nation" or the "glory of God." You won't know, you won't want to know *that what you're really building, day by day and hour by hour, is your own misery; that you don't understand your children, that you destroy their backbone before they can stand bravely erect; that you steal love; that you are money-mad and power-hungry; that you keep a dog because you're determined to be somebody's "master."* On through the centuries you'll repeat your mistakes until you and your kind die a mass death, victims of the universal social misery; until the horror of your existence strikes a first feeble spark of self-understanding in you. Then, very gradually, cautiously groping your way, you'll learn to seek out and to find your friend, the man of love, of work, and of knowledge. Then you will learn to understand, respect, and honor him. Then you will come to realize that a library is more essential to your life than a prize fight, that a contemplative stroll in the woods is better than parading, healing better than killing, self-reliance better than reliance on the nation, and soft-spoken modesty better than shouting, patriotic or otherwise.

You think the end justifies the means, however vile. I tell you: *The end is the means by which you achieve it.* Today's step is tomorrow's life. Great ends cannot be attained by base means. You've proved that in all your social upheavals. The meanness and inhumanity of the means make you mean and inhuman and make the end unattainable.

"How, then," I hear you ask, "shall I attain my end, whether it be Christian love, socialism, or American democracy?" Your Christian love and your socialism and your American democracy are what you do each day, your manner of thinking each hour, of embracing your life companion and loving your child; they are your attitude of *social responsibility* toward your work, and your determination not to become like the crushers of life you so hate.

But you, little man, abuse the freedom conferred on you by democratic institutions; you do your best to destroy these institutions instead of giving them a firm root in your daily life.

I've seen you as a German refugee abusing Swedish hospitality. At that time you were still a prospective leader of all the wretched of the earth. Do you remember the Swedish institution of smorgasbord? Oh yes, you do. You know what I mean! Can your memory be as short as all that? Then I'll remind you.

The Swedes have the generous custom of setting dishes filled with good things to eat on tables in their dining halls and leaving the guest free to take as much as he likes. To you this custom was strange and new. It was beyond you that anyone could put his trust in human decency. You told me with malicious glee that you had purposely gone without eating all day so as to be able to stuff yourself full of free food in the evening.

"I went hungry as a child . . ."

I know it, little man; I saw you go hungry and I know what hunger is. But what you don't know, you future savior of the prisoners of starvation, is that by stealing smorgasbord you are perpetuating your children's hunger a millionfold. There are certain things one just doesn't do. When receiving hospitality one does not steal silver spoons, or the host's wife, or his smorgasbord! After the downfall of Germany I saw you sitting on a park bench, half starved.

You told me that "Red Aid," the relief organization of your party of all the wretched of the earth, had refused to help you because you couldn't prove you were a party member. You'd lost your party card. Your leaders of all the hungry classify the hungry as red, white, and black. We, on the other hand, draw no distinctions: we recognize only one thing: the hungry organism.

That's what you're like in *little* things.

And in *big* things you're the same, little man.

You set out to banish capitalist exploitation from the world, to put an end to capitalist disregard for human life and to gain recognition of your rights. It's true that exploitation, contempt for human life, and ingratitude were with us a hundred years ago. But at that time there was also respect for great achievements, there were loyalty and gratitude toward the bestower of great benefits. When I look around me today, little man, I see you at work.

Where you have installed your own little leaders, the exploitation of your labor is more acute than a hundred years ago, the disregard for your life is more brutal, and certain rights that were formerly recognized have disappeared completely.

And where you're still fighting to install your own leaders, you've lost all respect for achievement; instead you steal the fruits of your great friends' hard work. You don't know what it is to recognize a benefit, because you think that if you were to recognize or respect anything you would no longer be a free American or Russian or Chinese. *What you wanted to destroy is flourishing more than ever, and what you should have preserved and guarded like your own life you've destroyed.* To you loyalty is "sentimentality" or a "petit-bourgeois habit"; respect for achievement is crawling servility. What you fail to notice is that you crawl where you should despise and are ungrateful where you should be loyal.

You see everything upside down, and you think that will take you to the land of freedom. You'll wake up from your nightmare, little man, and find yourself lying helpless on the ground, because you *steal from the giver and give to the thief*. You have mistaken the right of free speech and criticism for the right to shoot off your mouth and crack stupid jokes. You want to criticize but not to be criticized, and as a result you get torn to pieces and shot. You want to attack without exposing yourself to attack. That's why you always shoot from ambush.

"Police! Police! Is his passport in order? Is he really an M.D.? His name isn't in *Who's Who*, and the Medical Association is against him."

The police won't get you anywhere, little man. They can catch thieves and regulate traffic, but they can neither

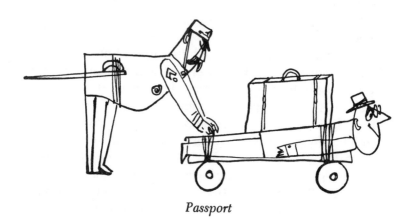

Passport

get you freedom nor safeguard it. You yourself have destroyed your freedom and you go on destroying it with deplorable consistency. Before the First World War there were no passports. You could cross any border you pleased without formalities. The war for "peace and freedom" introduced passports. If you wanted to travel two hundred miles in Europe, you had to apply to the consulates of ten different countries for permission. Today, after the second "war to end all wars," this is still the case, as it no doubt will be after the third and the eighth "war to end all wars."

"Did you hear that? He's casting aspersions on my martial spirit, on the honor and glory of my country!"

Be still, little man! There are two kinds of sound: the howling of the storm on a mountaintop, and your farting! You're a fart and you think you smell like violets. I heal your psychic affliction and you ask if I'm in *Who's Who*. I understand your cancer, and your little Health Commissioner forbids me to experiment on mice. I teach your physicians to understand your case, and your Medical Association denounces me to the police. You suffer from mental disorder and they apply electric shock, just as in the Middle Ages they would have applied the snake or the chain or the whip.

Better be still, little man! Your life is just too wretched. I can't hope to save you, but I'm going to finish what I have to say to you even if you come running, hooded and masked, with a rope in your cruel, bloody hand to hang me with. You can't hang me, little man, without hanging yourself. Because I am your life, your feeling for the world, your humanity, your love, and your joy in creating. No, you can't murder me, little man. I was once afraid of you, just as I once had too much faith in you. But since then I have soared above you. Today I see you in the perspective of the millennia, forward and backward in time. I want you to lose your fear of yourself. I want you to live more happily, more decently; I want you to be a living body instead of a rigid one, to love and not hate your children, to make your wife happy instead of subjecting her to "matrimonial" torment. I am your physician, and since you inhabit this planet, I am a planetary physician; I am neither a German, nor a Jew, nor a Christian, nor an Italian; I am a citizen of the earth. But you have eyes only for American angels and Japanese devils.

"Stop him! Investigate him! Has he got a license to practice medicine? Issue a royal decree forbidding him to practice without the consent of the king of our free country. He's carrying on experiments connected with my pleasure function! Throw him in jail! Deport him!"

I myself have acquired the right to carry on my work. No one can confer it on me. I have founded a new science which at long last makes it possible to understand you and your life. As certainly as for hundreds of years you have clutched at other doctrines as a last resort in your hour of peril, you will come back to mine in ten, a hundred, or a thousand years. Your Health Commissioner has no power over me, little man. He would be able to influence me only if he had the courage to recognize my truth. He hasn't got the courage. That's why, when he gets back to his own country, he announces that I have been interned in a mental hospital and why he appoints an ignoramus, who has tried to disprove the existence of the pleasure function by falsified experiments, Inspector General of Hospitals. But all this doesn't prevent me from writing this appeal to you, little man. Do you need further proof that your "authorities" are powerless? Your specialists, your health commissioners and professors have been unable to enforce their ban on the explanation of your cancer. They explicitly forbade me to study it and dissect it and subject it to microscopic analysis, but I went right ahead. Their trips to England and France to undermine my work proved futile. They're still bogged down in *pathology*. But I, little man, have often saved your life.

"When I raise my leaders of the world proletariat to power in Germany, I'll stand him against the wall! He has defamed our proletarian youth. He says the proletariat's capacity for love is as impaired as that of the bourgeoisie. He is turning my militant youth organizations into brothels. He says I'm an animal. He's destroying my class consciousness!"

Yes, I do destroy your ideals, those ideals that are costing you your reason and will cost you your life. You're unwilling to see your grand ideal except in a mirror, where you can't grab hold of it. *But only the truth in your own solid fist can make you the master of this earth!*

"Drive him out of the country! Make his life unbearable! He's undermining law and order. He's a spy in the pay of my deadly enemies! He's bought a house with Moscow (or Berlin) gold!"

You don't understand, little man! A little old woman was afraid of mice. She was afraid the mice would crawl under her skirt and between her legs. She wouldn't have had such a phobia if she had ever known love. She was my neighbor. She knew I had mice in the cellar. Through my work on these mice, I learned to understand your cancer. The poor little woman put pressure on you, little

man, who happened to be my landlord, to evict me. Armed with your great courage, your lofty idealism and morality, you gave me notice. I had to buy a house; that was the only way in which I could go on examining mice, unmolested by you and your cowardice. What did you do, little man? As an ambitious little district attorney you decided to use me, a prominent figure widely regarded as dangerous, to further your career. You said I was a German or a Russian spy. You had me arrested. But it was worth it to see you sitting there at my hearing, blushing to the roots of your hair. You were so pathetic I felt sorry for you. And when your secret agents searched my house for "incriminating material," the things they said about you weren't nice.

Later on, I met you again, this time in the person of a little Bronx judge with high ambitions and an uncertain future. You made a point of my having books by Lenin and Trotsky in my library. You didn't know what a library is for, little man. I told you to your face that I also had Hitler and Buddha and Jesus and Goethe and Napoleon and Casanova in my library, and explained that to understand the emotional plague one must examine it closely from all angles. That was news to you, little judge.

"Throw him in jail! He's a fascist! He despises the people!"

You're not the "people," little man. You're the one who despises the people, because you work not for *their* rights but for *your* career. This too has been told you by any number of greathearted men. But you've never read them, little man, I'm sure of that. I show respect for the people by incurring serious danger to tell them the truth. I could just as well play bridge with you and crack stupid jokes.

But I wouldn't sit at the same table with you. You are a poor advocate of the Declaration of Independence.

"He's a Trotskyite! Throw him in jail! The no-good Red, he's stirring up the people!"

Calm down, little man. I'm not stirring up the people, I'm trying to stir up your self-confidence and humanity, and you can't put up with that, because you want to make a career and win votes, so as to become a high-court judge or a leader of the world proletariat. Your justice and your leadership, little man, are a rope around the neck of mankind. What did you do to Woodrow Wilson, that great, warmhearted man? To you, if you're a judge in the Bronx, he was a "crazy idealist"; or if you're a coming leader of the world proletariat, he was a "capitalist bloodsucker." You murdered him, little man, murdered him with your indifference, your stupid talk, your fear of your hope.

You almost murdered me, little man!

Do you remember my laboratory ten years ago? I took you on as an assistant. You were unemployed. Someone had recommended you as an outstanding socialist, a member of the government party. You drew a good salary and were free in every sense of the word. I invited you to all our conferences, because I believed in you and your "mission." Do you remember, little man, what happened then? Freedom went to your head. Day after day, I saw you roaming around with your pipe in your mouth, doing nothing. Why weren't you working? I couldn't understand it. In the morning when I came into the lab, you waited provocatively for my greeting. I like to greet people first, little man. But when someone *waits* for my greeting, it makes me angry, because from *your* point of view I was

"Cancer research"

your "senior" and employer. I let you abuse your freedom for another few days. Then I had a talk with you. You tearfully admitted that you couldn't adjust to the new conditions. You weren't used to freedom. In your previous position you hadn't been allowed to smoke in your boss's presence; you'd been allowed to speak only when spoken to, you future leader of the world proletariat. And now that you were given *real* freedom, you became insolent and provocative. Because I understood you, I didn't fire you. Then you left and told some sexually abstinent court psychiatrist about my experiments. *You* were the secret informer, one of the contemptible hypocrites who un-leashed the newspaper campaign against me. That's what you're like, little man, when you're given freedom. But, contrary to your intention, your persecution advanced my work by ten years.

In view of all this, I'm bidding you goodbye, little man. I will serve you no more, I refuse to let my concern for you torture me slowly to death. You can't follow me to the distant places I'm bound for. You'd be scared to death if you so much as suspected what the future has in store for you—because undoubtedly you're in the process of inherit-ing the earth, little man! My remote solitudes are a part of your future. But for the present I don't want you as a traveling companion. As a traveling companion you may be all right in a club car, but not where I'm going.

"Kill him! He despises the civilization that I, the little man in the street, have built. I'm a free citizen of a free democracy. Hurrah!"

You're nothing, little man! Nothing whatever! You didn't build this civilization, it was built by a few of your more decent masters. Even if you're a builder, you don't know what you're building. If I or someone else were to say, "Take responsibility for what you're building," you'd call me a traitor to the proletariat and flock to the Father of all Proletarians, who does *not* say such things.

You're not free, little man, and you haven't the faintest idea what freedom is. You wouldn't know how to live in freedom. Who brought the plague to power in Europe? You, little man! And in America? Think of Wilson!

"Listen to him! He's accusing *me*, the little man! Who am I? What power have I to interfere with the President of the United States? I do my duty and obey orders. I don't meddle with politics."

When you drag thousands of men, women, and children to the gas chambers, you're only obeying orders. Is that right, little man? And you're so innocent you don't even know that such things are happening. And you're only a poor devil, whose opinion counts for nothing, who hasn't even got one. And who are you, anyway, that you should meddle with politics? I know, I know! I've heard all that many times. But then I ask: Why don't you do your duty in silence when a wise man tells you that you and you alone are responsible for what you do, or tries to persuade you not to beat your children, or pleads with you for the thousandth time to stop obeying dictators? What becomes of your duty, your innocent obedience, then? No, little man, when truth speaks, you don't listen. You listen only to bluster. And then you shout Hurrah! Hurrah! You're cowardly and cruel, little man; you have no sense of your true duty, which is to be a *man* and to preserve *humanity*. You imitate wise men so badly and bandits so well. Your movies and radio programs are full of murder.

You will drag yourself and your meanness through many centuries before becoming your own master. I'm bidding you goodbye in order to work more effectively for your future, because when I'm far away you can't kill me, and you respect my work more in the distance than close at hand. *You despise anything that's too close to you!* That's why you put your proletarian general or marshal on a pedestal; then, however contemptible he may be, you can respect him. And that's why great men have given you a wide berth since the dawn of history.

You put your general on a pedestal;
then you can respect him

"That's megalomania. The man is stark raving mad!"

I know, little man, you're very quick to diagnose madness when a truth doesn't suit you. You regard yourself as "normal"! You've locked up the lunatics and the world is run by you normal people. Then who's to blame for all the trouble? Not you, of course; you only do your duty, and who are you to have an opinion of your own? I know. You don't have to say it again. It's not you I'm worried about, little man! But when I think of your children, when I think how you torment the life out of them trying to make them "normal" like yourself, I almost want to come back to you and do what I can to stop your crimes. But I also know that you've taken precautions against that by appointing commissioners of education and child care.

I wish I could take you on a little tour of the world, little man, to show you what you, as the "apostle and embodiment of the people," are and have been, in the present and in the past, in Vienna, London, and Berlin. You'd find yourself everywhere and recognize yourself without difficulty, regardless of whether you're a Frenchman, a

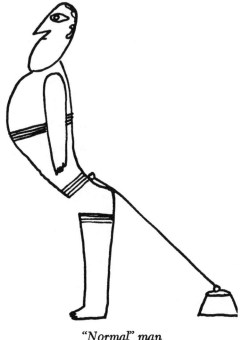

"Normal" man

When I think of your children,
how you torment the life out of them,
trying to make them "normal" like yourself . . .

German, or a Hottentot, if only you had the courage to look at yourself.

"He's insulting me, he's desecrating my mission!"

I'm not insulting you, little man, and I'm not desecrating your mission. I'll be only too glad if you show me I'm wrong, if you *prove* that you're capable of looking at yourself and recognizing yourself, if you can give me the same kind of proofs as I'd expect of a mason who's building a house. I'd expect him to show me that the house exists and is fit to live in. And if I prove that instead of building houses he merely talks about his "mission to build houses," this mason will hardly be entitled to accuse me of insulting him. In the same light, it's up to you to prove that you are the apostle and the embodiment of man's future. It's no use trying to hide like a coward behind the "honor" of the nation, or of the proletariat, because you've already shown too much of your true nature.

I say it again: I'm bidding you goodbye. It's taken me many years and cost me a good many sleepless, tormented nights. Your coming leaders of the world proletariat don't make things so hard for themselves. Today they're your leaders and tomorrow you'll find them grinding out copy for some nondescript weekly. They change their opinions as easily as a man changes his shirt. I don't change my opinions as if they were dirty shirts. I keep faith with you and your future. But since you're incapable of respecting anyone you rub shoulders with, I'm obliged to get away from you. Your great-grandchildren will inherit my efforts. I know that, and I don't mind waiting for them to enjoy the fruits of my labors, just as I've been waiting for thirty years for you to accept and make use of them. But all you do is shout "Hurrah, hurrah" or "Down with capitalism" or "Down with the Constitution."

Some hundred years ago, echoing the physicists and machine builders, you began to babble that the soul doesn't exist. Then a great man came and showed you your soul, but he wasn't able to tell you how this soul is anchored in your body. You said: "Psychoanalysis is absurd! It's charlatanism! Urine can be analyzed, not the soul." You were able to talk like that because all you saw in medicine was urine analysis. The struggle for your soul went on for forty hard years. I know that struggle because I took part in it for your sake. One day you found out that you could make a lot of money out of the diseased human soul. It sufficed to have a mental patient spend an hour a day with you for several years, and to charge him so much an hour.

Then and not a moment sooner did you become convinced that the soul exists. In the meantime, the study of your perishable body proceeded quietly. I discovered that your soul is a function of your life energy; in other words, that body and soul are a unity. By following this clue, I further discovered that your life energy stretches out when you feel happy and loving and contracts when you are suffering from anxiety. For fifteen years you ignored me. But I continued along the same lines and discovered that this life energy, which I called "orgone," also exists in the atmosphere outside your body. I succeeded in seeing it in the dark and in devising an apparatus with which to magnify it and make it visible in flashes. For two years, while you were playing cards or talking political nonsense, or tormenting your wife or ruining your child, I was spending many hours a day in the dark, verifying my discovery of your life energy. Little by little I found a way of demonstrating it to others, and it became evident that they saw the same thing as I did.

And now, if you happen to be a doctor who believes the psyche to be a secretion of the endocrine glands, you tell one of the patients I have been able to cure that my success was due to "suggestion." If you happen to suffer from obsessive doubts and to be afraid of the dark, you say the phenomenon you have just observed was a product of suggestion and that you felt as if you were attending a spiritualist séance. That's the way you are, little man! In 1946 you're making preposterous assertions about the soul as confidently as you denied its existence in 1920. You're still the same little man. In 1984 you won't hesitate to make money out of the orgone and to slander, ridicule, and belittle some other truth, just as you have slandered, ridiculed, and belittled the discovery of the soul or of the cosmic energy. And you will go right on being the little man, the "critical" little man, ubiquitously shouting hurrah, hurrah. Do you remember how you ridiculed the discovery that the earth does not stand still but rotates on its axis and revolves around the sun, by saying that if this were true the glasses on a waiter's tray would totter and fall off. That was a few hundred years ago, little man. Of course you've forgotten. All you know about Newton is that he saw an apple falling from a tree, and of Rousseau that he wanted to go "back to nature." From Darwin you took only the "struggle for existence," but not the fact that you are descended from the ape. And of Goethe's *Faust*, which you're so fond of quoting, you understand no more than a cat understands of mathematics. You are stupid and vain, empty and apelike, little man. With a deadly certainty you miss the essential and cling to the fallacy. I've told you that before. In your bookstores you display deluxe editions of books about your Napoleon, that little man in gold braid who left the world nothing but universal conscription, but in none of your bookstores is it possible to find a copy of my Kepler with his early intimation of your cosmic origins. That's why you are and remain in the muck, little man. That's why you persist in believing that I spent twenty years of worry and pains, not to mention money, trying to convince you of the existence of cosmic energy by "suggestion." No, little man, in sacrificing so much, I actually learned to heal the plague in your body. You don't believe me. In Norway I heard you say, "Anybody who spends so much money on experiments is literally mad." I understood you. You judge me by yourself. *You can only take, you can't give.* That's why it's no more conceivable to you that a man might find his greatest joy in giving than that it might be possible to spend three minutes with a member of the opposite sex without starting to f . . .

You steal the benefits of life. I'd respect you if you were a big thief, but you're a small, cowardly thief. You're shrewd and adroit, but because your mind is constipated you can't create. So you steal a bone and crawl away to gnaw at it. Freud once told you as much. You gather around the willing, joyful giver and suck him dry. You suck and in your perversity you call him the "sucker." *You cram yourself full of his knowledge, his happiness, his greatness, but you can't digest what you've eaten.* It comes right out in shit and stinks abominably. Or to preserve your dignity after your theft, you revile the victim, calling him a madman or a charlatan or a seducer of children.

Yes, a "seducer of children"! Do you remember, little man (you were the president of a scientific organization at the time), how you slandered me, telling people that I encouraged my children to watch the sexual act? I had just published my first paper on the genital rights of children. And another time, do you remember (you happened at the moment to be president of an "association for some sort of culture" in Berlin) how you spread the rumor that I took teenage girls out to the woods in my car to seduce them. I have never seduced a teenage girl, little man.

That's *your* dirty mind, not mine. I love my wife or my woman; I'm not like you, who dream of seducing little girls in the woods because you're unable to love your wife.

And you, little adolescent girl, don't you dream about some movie star? Don't you take his picture to bed with you at night? Don't you sneak up to him, claiming to be over eighteen, and seduce him? And then what? Don't you hale your movie star into court and accuse him of rape? He's either acquitted or convicted and your grandmothers kiss the great movie star's hands! You understand, little girl!

You wanted to sleep with the famous movie star, but you hadn't the courage to do it on your own responsibility, so you put the blame on him, you poor raped little thing. Or, for that matter, you poor raped woman, who experienced more pleasure with your chauffeur than with your husband. Didn't you seduce your Negro chauffeur, whose sexuality was still close to the African jungle? Didn't you, little white woman? And afterward didn't you accuse him of rape, you poor helpless thing, you "victim of primitive bestiality"? No, of course not, you were pure and white, a member of the "Daughters of This, That, or the Other Revolution," a Northerner or a Southerner, whose grandfather got rich dragging African Negroes from the free jungle to America in chains! How innocent, how pure, how white, how far from any desire for black flesh, you poor little woman! You miserable coward, you monstrous product of a sick race of slave hunters, you descendant of the cruel Cortés, who lured thousands of trusting Aztecs into a trap and shot them down.

Ah, you poor daughters of this, that, and the other

revolution! What do you know of the yearnings of the fathers of the American Revolution, or of Lincoln, who freed your slaves—whereupon you promptly threw them on the "free market" of supply and demand. Look at yourselves in the mirror, you chaste, innocent daughters of the red-white-and-blue revolution. Do you know what you'll see? A "daughter of the Russian Revolution"!

If you had *just once been able to give a man love,* the lives of a good many Negroes, Jews, and workers would have been saved. Just as in children you kill what is alive in yourselves, so in Negroes you murder your own intimations of love, your pleasure fantasies that have degenerated into frivolous pornography. What abysmal meanness your deadened sex organs breed! No, you daughter of this, that, and the other revolution, I have no desire to become a district attorney or a commissar. I leave that to your rigid animals in robes and uniforms. I love my birds

Daughter of this, that, and the other revolution

and my deer and my badgers, which are close to the Negroes. I mean the jungle Negroes, not the ones in Harlem with their stiff collars and zoot suits. Not the fat bejeweled Negresses, whose frustrated desire has been converted into excess flesh or religion. I mean the slender, supple bodies of the South Sea Island girls who let themselves be fucked by you, the sexual pigs of this, that, and the other army, unaware that you draw no distinction between their pure love and what you'd expect to find in a Denver brothel.

Yes, little white woman, you crave a living being who has not yet understood that he's exploited and despised. Though your German counterpart, the daughter of the Germanic race, has ceased to function, you're still with us as a Russian daughter of the triumphant working class or as a Daughter of the American Revolution. But in five hundred or a thousand years, when healthy young men and women with healthy bodies have learned to cherish love and to safeguard it, nothing will remain of you but a ludicrous memory.

Haven't you, you little cancerous woman, denied your concert halls to Marian Anderson, who is the very voice of life? Long after all trace of you will have vanished from this planet, Marian Anderson's name will be singing to the centuries. I can't help wondering whether Marian Anderson also *thinks* centuries ahead, or whether she forbids her child to enjoy love. I don't know. Life has its own rhythms and seasons. It contents itself with those who let it live and has no need of you, cancerous little lady.

You've propagated the myth that *you* are "society," little woman, and your little man has swallowed it. You are *not* society. Yes, you announce every day in the big Jewish and Christian newspapers that your daughter is about to embrace a man, but nobody in his right mind is interested. "Society" is the carpenter and the mason and the gardener and the teacher and the doctor and the factory worker and myself. We are society and not you, you rigid, cancerous, masklike woman! You're not life, you're its greatest curse. But I understand why you've shut yourself up in your fortress with all your money. In view of the smallness of the carpenters and gardeners and doctors and teachers and masons and factory workers, no other course was open to you. In the midst of this plague, it was the wisest thing you ever did. But what with your constipation, your gout, your mask, your negation of life, smallness has become second nature to you. You're unhappy, poor little woman, because your sons go to the dogs, your daughters grow up to be whores, your husband dries up, your life rots and your tissues with it. You can't tell *me* any fairy tales, little daughter of the revolution. I've seen you naked!

You've always been a coward, daughter of this, that, and the other revolution. You had the happiness of mankind in the palm of your hand and you frittered it away. You've brought Presidents into the world and taught them triviality. They hand out medals and get their pictures taken; they smile their everlasting smiles, and they're afraid to look life in the face, you little daughter of the revolution. You had the world in the palm of your hand, and what did you do? You dropped your atom bombs on Hiroshima and Nagasaki; that is, your son dropped the bombs as a sample of things to come. What you dropped, little cancerous woman, was your tombstone. With those two bombs you bombed your whole class and race into the tomb for all time! Because you hadn't the humanity to warn the men and women and children of Hiroshima and Nagasaki. And because you were too small to be human, you will perish as silently as a stone sinks into the sea. It doesn't matter in the least what you think and say now, little woman who has brought idiotic generals into the world. In five hundred years you'll be remembered only as a curiosity and laughingstock. If that's not the universal opinion of you today, it's only one more sign of the wretched state of the world.

I know, I know, little woman. All the appearances are in your favor; you were fighting for your country, and so on. I heard that once long ago in Austria. Did you ever hear a Vienna hack driver shouting, "Long live my emperor!"? No? It doesn't matter. Just listen to yourself; it's the same tune. No, little woman, I'm not afraid of you. You can't do anything to me. I know, your son-in-law is a district attorney or your nephew is a tax collector in my town. You ask him to tea and slip in an indignant word about me. He's eager for a promotion and looking for a victim, somebody he can sacrifice to law and order. I know how it's done. But that won't save you, little woman. My truth is stronger than you.

"He's biased! He's a fanatic! Haven't I any function in society at all?"

I've only told you in what ways you are *small* and *mean*, little man and little woman. I haven't said a word about your usefulness or importance. Do you think I'd risk my life talking to you if you weren't important? Your importance, your enormous responsibility, makes your meanness all the more monstrous. You're said to be stupid. I say you're shrewd but *cowardly*. You're said to be the manure needed to fertilize human society. I say you're the seed.

It is said that culture requires slaves. I say that no cultured society can be built with slaves. This terrible twentieth century has made all cultural theories from Plato down seem ridiculous. *Little man, there has never been a human culture.* We're barely beginning to understand the awful deviation and pathological degeneration of the human animal. This appeal to the little man or anything else that can be said on the subject today, however wise and well-intentioned, bears no more resemblance to the culture that will develop in a thousand or five thousand years than does the first wheel contrived thousands of years ago to a modern diesel locomotive.

Your thinking is shortsighted, little man; you can see no farther than from breakfast to lunch. You must learn to think backward and forward over the centuries. You must learn to think in terms of life as a whole, of *your* development from the first plasmatic flake to the human animal who walks upright but continues to think in twists and turns. Because you have no memory for things that happened ten or twenty years ago, you're still mouthing the same nonsense as two thousand years ago. Worse, you cling with might and main to such absurdities as "race," "class," "nation," and the obligation to observe a religion and repress your love. You're afraid to acknowledge the depth of your wretchedness. From time to time you lift your head out of the muck and shout Hurrah! A frog croaking in a swamp is closer to life.

"Why don't you save me from the muck? Why don't you attend my party meetings and political conferences? You're a renegade. In former days you fought and suffered and made sacrifices for me. Now you insult me."

I can't save you from the muck. Only you can do that.

From time to time you lift your head
out of the muck and shout Hurrah!

I've never participated in party meetings or political conferences because all they do is shout, "Down with the main point!" and "Hurrah for incidentals!" It's true that I fought for you for twenty-five years at the sacrifice of my family life and professional security; I gave your organizations a lot of money and took part in your demonstrations and hunger marches. It's true that as a physician I gave you thousands of hours of my time without pay, and it's true that I was driven from country to country for you and often in your stead, while you were shouting hurrah at the top of your lungs. I was literally ready to die for you. In the struggle against the political plague I drove you around in my car, though I myself was threatened with the death penalty. In demonstrations I helped to protect your children against the assaults of the police. I spent all my money setting up mental-health clinics where you could go for help and advice. But all you did was take; you never gave anything in return. You wanted only to be saved, and in thirty dreadful plague years you never had one fruitful idea. And when the Second World War was over, you were right back where you were when it started, a little further to the "left" or "right," but you hadn't *advanced* a single millimeter! You frittered away the great French liberation, and you transformed the still greater Russian liberation into the world's greatest nightmare. Your failure—your terrible failure, which only great, lonely hearts can understand without anger or contempt—has driven to despair all those who were prepared to make every sacrifice for you. For in all those terrible years, in that murderous half century, not a single reasonable, salutary word came out of your mouth, but only slogans.

Still, I didn't lose heart, because in the meantime I had gained a better and deeper understanding of your sickness. I knew that you couldn't have thought or acted any differently. I recognized your panic fear of everything that's alive in you. It's that fear which always leads you astray, even when you've made a good start. You simply fail to realize that *hope* must spring from your own understanding. You pump hope only into yourself, never out of yourself. That, little man, is why, considering the utter rottenness of your own world, you call me an "optimist." Yes, I *am* optimistic, full of the future. How is that possible? I'll tell you.

As long as I cared about you, your obstinacy struck me one blow after another. A thousand times I forgot how you had rewarded me for helping you, and a thousand times you reminded me that you were sick. Then one day I opened my eyes and looked you straight in the face. At first I felt a surge of contempt and hatred. But little

Then one day I opened my eyes and looked you straight in the face

by little I learned to let my *understanding* of your sickness counteract my hatred and contempt. After that I was no longer angry at you for making such a mess of the world in your first attempts at world leadership. It became clear to me that just this was bound to happen, because for thousands of years you had been prevented from living in any true sense.

My dear little man, I was discovering the functional law of life while you were shouting from the rooftops, "He's crazy!" At that time you happened to be a little psychiatrist with a past in the youth movement and, due to your impotence, a cardiac future. Later on you died of a broken heart, for no man can steal or slander with impunity, not if he has an ounce of integrity. And that you had, tucked away in a corner of your soul. When you thought I was done for, you ceased to be my friend and became my enemy. You tried to give me the *coup de grâce* because, though you knew I was right, you were unable to keep pace with me. And then when I bobbed up like a jumping jack, stronger, more clear-sighted, more resolute than ever, you died of fright. Before you died, you saw that I had leaped headlong over towering barriers, some of which you yourself had raised in your desire to destroy me. Didn't you, in your pussyfooting organization, pass off *my* teachings as your own? I assure you that the honest members were aware of this. I know, because they told me. Underhanded tactics, little man, can only bring you to your grave before your time.

It's dangerous to be with you; in your company a man cannot remain faithful to the truth without fear of calumny and violence. That's why I withdrew—not, I repeat, from your future but from your present, not from your humanity but from your inhumanity and meanness.

I'm still prepared for any sacrifice, but only for *life,* not for you, little man! It was only recently that I saw the enormous mistake I made twenty-five years ago. I had been devoting my life to you in the belief that you were life, that you were hope and integrity, that you were the future. Many true and upright men have sought life in you, and all have perished. When this became clear to me, I resolved not to die a victim of your narrowness and smallness. For I have important work to do. Little man, *I have discovered the energy that is life.* And I no longer confuse you with the force that I sensed in myself and looked for in you.

Only if I distinguish your character and behavior, little man, clearly and sharply from those of one who is truly alive, shall I be able to make a great contribution to the security of life and to *your* future. It takes courage to disavow you, that I know. But I also know that I shall be able to go on working for the future because I don't pity you and because I have no desire to become a little big man through you, as your contemptible leaders have done.

The life-force in man has long been maltreated, but only recently has it begun to fight back. This is a great beginning toward your great future and gives promise of a terrible end to every kind of smallness in little men!

We have found out how the emotional plague operates. Having decided to gobble up Poland, it accuses Poland of planning armed aggression. Having decided to murder a rival, it accuses him of plotting murder. Having contrived some pornographic enormity, it accuses the healthy of sexual depravity.

We've caught on to you, little man; we've looked behind

your pathetic mask and seen through your pleas for sympathy. We want you to build the future with your *work* and your achievement; we don't want you to replace a bad tyrant with one who is still worse. More and more resolutely, little man, we are beginning to demand of you, as you demand of others, that you submit to the rules of life, and that you expend as much effort in improving yourself as you do in criticizing others. We are learning more and more about your greed, your irresponsibility, your passion for gossip; in short, your all-embracing sickness that is stinking up this fair world of ours. I know; I know you don't like to hear this; you'd rather shout hurrah, you embodiment of the future Workers' Fatherland or Fourth Reich. But I don't believe you'll be as successful in contaminating the world as you've been in the past. We've found the key to your millennial secret. You're a brute behind your mask of sociability and friendliness, little man. You can't spend an hour with me without giving yourself away. You don't believe me? Let me refresh your memory.

Do you remember the fine sunny afternoon when, in the person of a woodsman, you came to my house looking for work. You saw my young dog, who sniffed you lovingly and jumped up on you full of joy. You saw he had the makings of a fine hunting dog and said. "Chain him up to make him vicious! This dog is too friendly." I answered: "I don't want a vicious chained dog. I don't like ferocious dogs." I have a lot more enemies in this world than you, you friendly little woodsman, and nevertheless I prefer a sweet-tempered dog who is friendly to strangers.

Do you remember the dismal, rainy Sunday when worry over your biological rigidity drove me out to a bar? I was sitting there drinking whiskey—no, little man, I'm not a

You're a brute behind your mask
of sociability and friendliness

drinker, though I like a drink of whiskey now and then. Anyway, I was drinking a highball. You were slightly tipsy, you'd been in the war and had just come home from overseas. You described the Japanese as "ugly-looking apes." And then with that peculiar facial expression that I have purposely provoked in my treatment room in an effort to cure your plague, you said: "You know what we ought to do to those Japs on the West Coast? String 'em up, every last one of them. But not quickly; no, *very slowly*, twisting the noose a little tighter every five minutes . . . very slowly . . . like this . . ." And you twisted your hand to illustrate your meaning, little man. The waiter nodded his approval and admired your heroic virility. Have you ever held a little Japanese baby in your arms, you little patriot? No? On through the centuries you'll keep stringing up Japanese spies and American fliers and Russian peasant women and German officers and English anarchists and Greek Communists; you'll shoot them, electrocute them, and asphyxiate them in gas chambers, but all that won't make the slightest change in the constipation of your bowels and mind, in your incapacity for love, your rheumatism and psychic disorder. No amount of shooting or hanging will pull you out of the muck you're in. Take a look at yourself, little man! That's your only hope.

And little woman, do you remember the day when you were sitting in my office, talking venomously about your husband, who had just left you? For years you and your mother and your aunts and your great-nephews and cousins had been sitting on him so heavily that he was beginning to shrivel up. He'd been having to provide for you and all your relations. In a last stirring of his life-feeling, he finally tore himself away and came to me for help, because he wasn't strong enough to free himself from you inwardly by his own resources. He willingly paid you alimony, three quarters of his income as prescribed by an abominable law. That was the price of his freedom from oppression, and he didn't begrudge it because he was a great artist and neither art nor true science can live in chains. Though you had learned a profession, you wanted only to be supported by the man you bitterly hated. You knew that I would help him to free himself from unwarranted obligations and that made you furious. You threatened me with the police. I was only trying to help the man in his dire need, but you said I wanted to take all his money for myself. In other words, poor little woman, you credited me with your evil intentions. It never occurred to you to develop your aptitude for your profession. That would have made you independent, independent of the man for whom you had long had no other feeling than hate. Do you think you can build a new world in such a way? I heard you had socialist friends, who "knew all about me." Don't you see that you're a *type,* that there are millions of your kind and that you are destroying the world? I know, I know. You're weak and lonely, you're "tied" to your mother, you're "helpless." You yourself hate your hatred, you can't stand yourself, and you're desperate. And that, little woman, is why you destroy your husband's life. And you drift along with the stream of life as it is today. I also know that you have a good many judges and district attorneys on your side, but believe me they have no answer to your misery.

I see and hear you, little woman, in the person of a stenographer in some government building, taking notes on my past and present and future, my political outlook and my opinions about private property and Russia and democracy. I'm asked about my social status. I reply that I hold honorary membership in three scientific and literary societies, including the International Society for Plasmogeny. The examiner is impressed. At our next session he says to me, "Here's something odd. It says in the record that you're an honorary member of the International Society for *Polygamy*." And we both laugh at your little mistake. Now do you know how I've come by my honors and dishonors, little woman of the wild fantasies? Thanks to your fantasies, not to my mode of life. Isn't it true that all you remember about Rousseau is that he wanted to go "back to nature," that he neglected his children and sent them to an orphan asylum? You're malicious to the bottom of your soul; your thoughts pass the beautiful by and come to rest on the ugly!

"Listen, all you righteous citizens! I've seen him drawing his curtains at 1 a.m. What can he be doing? And all day long his curtains are wide open. There must be something at the bottom of it!"

It won't help you any longer to use such methods against the truth. We know all about them. You're not interested in my curtains, you're interested in stopping my truth. You want to go on being an informer and a slanderer, you want to go on sending your innocent neighbor to jail if his way of life doesn't suit you, because he's kindly or free, because he works and doesn't bother his head about you. You're very curious, little man, you snoop and slander. Luckily for you, the police never inform on their informers.

"Listen, fellow taxpayers! He's a professor of philosophy. A great university wants to employ him to instruct the young. It's an outrage! Down with him! Hurrah for the taxpayers! Let them decide who is to teach and who isn't!"

Whereupon your righteous housewife, also a taxpayer, sends in a petition against this teacher of truth and he doesn't get the job. Little housewife and taxpayer, righteous mother of patriots, you have proved more powerful than four thousand years of philosophy and science. But we're beginning to understand you. And sooner or later your righteous machinations will be stopped.

"Listen, listen, ye faithful guardians of public morality! There, around the corner, a mother is living with her

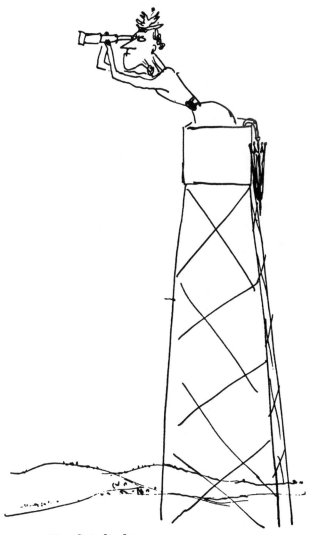

Moralist checking up on orgone energy

daughter. The daughter has a boy friend who goes to see her late at night. Have the mother arrested for procuring! Call the police! In the interests of morality, law, and order!"

And this mother is punished because you, you prurient little man, go poking your nose into other people's beds. You've shown yourself up. We know the motive behind your "morality, law, and order." Aren't you always trying to make passes at waitresses? *Yes, we want our sons and daughters to enjoy their love openly and not, as you would like them to, in dark corners.* We honor those courageous fathers and mothers who understand their adolescent sons' and daughters' love, and protect it. Such mothers and fathers are the seed from which will grow the generations of the future, healthy in body and mind, untainted by your scatological fantasies, you little impotent man of the twentieth century!

"Listen, fellow citizens! Have you heard the latest? He's a homosexual. He assaulted one of his patients and the poor man fled with his pants down."

Admit that you drool with lust as you tell this "true story." Do you know where it came from? It grew from the manure pile inside you, from your filthy, diseased nature, your constipation and your loathsome desires. I've never had homosexual desires, like you, little man; I've never wanted to seduce little girls, like you, little man; I've never raped a woman, like you, little man, and I've never suffered from constipation, like you, little man. I've never embraced a woman unless she wanted me and I wanted her, and I've never stolen love, like you, little man. I've never exhibited myself in public as you do, little man, and I haven't got a scatological imagination, like you, little man!

"Have you heard about this? He molested his secretary so much that she ran out on him. He'd been living alone with her in the *same house*, his curtains were drawn and the light was on in his room until three in the morning!"

You said that La Mettrie was a voluptuary who choked to death on a pasty. The spittle ran down your jowls as you spoke of Crown Prince Rudolph's morganatic marriage. You said that Eleanor Roosevelt wasn't quite normal, that the President of X University had caught his wife *in flagrante*, and that the village schoolteacher had a lover.

Investigating the orgone accumulator

Didn't you say all that, little man? Oh, you wretched, miserable citizen of this planet, who have been frittering away your life for thousands of years and are still up to your ears in muck!

"Arrest him! He's a German spy! It wouldn't surprise me if he were a Russian spy and an Icelandic spy to boot. I saw him on Eighty-sixth Street in New York at three o'clock in the afternoon. What's more, he had a woman with him!"

Do you know, little man, how a bedbug looks under the Northern Lights? No? I didn't think so! Someday there will be strict laws against your bedbuggishness, little man, severe *laws for the protection of truth and love!* Today you throw adolescent lovers in jail, but someday *you* will be sent to a house of reflection for smearing decent people with your filth. There will be a new kind of judge and lawyer; their stock-in-trade will not be the formalistic pettifoggery of today, but truth, justice, and kindness. There will be laws, *severe laws for the protection of life,* and you will have to obey them, little man, though you'll hate them. I know: you'll go on with your emotional plague, your slander and intrigue, your diplomatic maneuvers and inquisitions for three or five or ten centuries more. But in the end, little man, you'll be defeated. You'll be defeated by your own feeling for cleanliness, which today you keep blocked up deep inside you.

No kaiser, no tsar, no father of the world proletariat has conquered you! They have enslaved you, but *none has been able to rob you of your meanness. What will get the better of you in the end, little man, is your feeling for cleanliness, your yearning for life. Of that there is no doubt!* Cleansed of your smallness and meanness, you'll begin to *think*. At first your thinking will be pitiful and misguided; but you will be seriously thinking. Your thinking will cause you suffering and you'll learn to bear it, just as I and others have had to grit our teeth and bear the suffering provoked by our thinking *about you* for years on end. Our sufferings on your account will make you think. And once you've started to think, you'll be amazed at your last four thousand years of "civilization." You'll wonder how you could have put up with newspapers full of nothing but receptions, parades and medals, prosecutions and executions, foreign policy, Realpolitik and diplomatic skulduggery, mobilization, demobilization and re-mobilization, nonaggression pacts, drilling and bombing. You absorbed that stuff with the patience of an enslaved sheep. If you had stopped there, you might still have understood yourself. But no, for centuries you took it up, you echoed it. You distrusted your own sound ideas and accepted the false ideas you read in the papers, because you thought they were patriotic. And that, little man, is something it will take you a long time to get over. You will be ashamed of your history, and the only hope is that to our great-great-grandchildren the study of history will no longer be a torment. It will no longer be possible to carry out a great revolution in order to go back to Peter "the Great."

A GLIMPSE OF THE FUTURE. I can't tell you what your future will be. I have no way of knowing whether you'll ever get to the moon or to Mars with the help of the cosmic orgone I have discovered. Nor can I know how your space ships will take off or land, whether you will light your houses with solar energy, or whether

you will be able to talk with someone in Australia or
Baghdad through a slit in the wall of your room. But I can
tell you what you will definitely *not* do in five hundred
or a thousand or five thousand years.

"Would you listen to that! He's a crank! He can tell
me what I won't do! Is he a dictator?"

I'm not a dictator, little man, though, what with your
smallness, I might easily have become one. Your dictators
can tell you only what you *can't* do in the present without
ending up in a gas chamber. They can no more tell you
what you will do in the distant future than they can make
a tree grow faster.

"But where do *you* get your wisdom, you intellectual
servant of the revolutionary proletariat?"

From your own depths, you eternal proletarian of human reason!

"Listen to that! He gets his wisdom from *my* depths!
I haven't got any depths. And what kind of individualistic
talk is this, anyway!!"

Oh yes, little man, you have depths, but you don't
know it. You're afraid, mortally afraid of your depths;
that's why you neither feel them nor see them. That's
why your head swims when you look into the depths,
why you reel as if you were on the edge of a precipice.
You're afraid of falling and losing your "special character."
Because, try as you will to find yourself, it's always the
same cruel, envious, greedy, thieving little man that turns
up. I wouldn't have written this long appeal to you, little
man, if you didn't have deep depths. And I know these
depths in you, little man, because in my work as a physician I discovered them when you came to me with your

114

affliction. Your depths are your great future. And that is why I can tell you what you will certainly not do in the future. A time will come when you won't even understand how you were able, in these four thousand years of un-culture, to do all the things you have done. Now will you listen to me?

"Why shouldn't I listen to a nice little utopia? In any case, nothing can be done about it, my dear Doctor. I'll always be the little man of the people with no opinion of my own. And anyway, who am I to . . . ?"

Just be still! You're hiding behind the myth of the little man, because you're afraid of getting into the stream of life and of *having* to swim—if only for the sake of your children and grandchildren.

All right. The first of all the many things you will *not* do in the future is to regard yourself as a little man with no opinion of his own, who says, "Anyway, who am I to . . . ?" You *have* an opinion of your own and in the future you will regard it as a disgrace *not* to know it, *not* to express it and stand up for it.

"But what will public opinion say about my opinion? I'll be crushed like a worm if I express my own opinion!"

What you call "public opinion," little man, is the aggregate of all the opinions of little men and women. Every little man and every little woman has inside him a sound opinion of his own and a particular kind of unsound opinion. Their unsound opinions spring from the fear of the unsound opinions of all the other little men and women. That's why the sound opinions don't come to light. For instance, you will no longer believe that you "count for nothing." You will know and proclaim that you are the mainstay and foundation of this human society. Don't run away! Don't be afraid! It's not so bad to be a responsible mainstay of human society.

"What then must I do in order to be the mainstay of society?"

Nothing new or unusual. Just go on doing what you're already doing: till your field, wield your hammer, examine your patient, take your children out playing or to school, write articles about the events of the day, investigate the secrets of nature. You're already doing all these things, but you think they're unimportant and that only what Marshal Medalchest or Prince Blowhard says or does is important.

"You're a dreamer, Doctor. Don't you see that Marshal Medalchest and Prince Blowhard have the soldiers and the arms needed to make war, to mobilize me for their war, and to blow my field, my factory, my laboratory, or my office to pieces?"

You get yourself mobilized, your field and your factory are blown to pieces, because you shout hurrah, hurrah when they mobilize you and blow your factory and field to pieces. Prince Blowhard would have neither soldiers nor arms if you really knew that a field was for growing wheat and a factory for making furniture or shoes, that fields and factories were not made to be blown to pieces, and if you stood foursquare behind your knowledge. Your Marshal Medalchest and your Prince Blowhard don't know these things. They themselves don't work in a field, factory, or office. They think you work not to feed and clothe your children but for the grandeur of the German or the Workers' Fatherland.

"Then what should I do? I hate war; my wife cries

her heart out when I'm drafted, my children starve when the proletarian armies occupy my land, corpses pile up by the millions . . . All I want to do is till my field and play with the children after work, love my wife at night, and dance, sing, and make music on holidays. What should I do?"

Just go on doing what you've been doing and wanting to do all along: work, let your children grow up happily, love your wife at night. *If you stuck to this program knowingly and single-mindedly there would be no war.* Your wife wouldn't be fair game for the sex-starved soldiers of the Workers' Fatherland, your orphaned children wouldn't starve in the streets, and you yourself wouldn't end up staring glassy-eyed at the blue sky on some far-off "field of honor."

"But supposing I want to live for my work and my wife and my children, what can I do if the Huns or Germans or Japanese or Russians or somebody else marches in, and forces me to make war? I have to defend my house and home, don't I?"

Right you are, little man. If the Huns of any nation attack you, you've got to pick up your gun. But what you fail to see is that the "Huns" of all nations are simply millions of little men like yourself who persist in shouting hurrah, hurrah when Prince Blowhard (who doesn't work) calls them to the colors; little men like yourself who believe that they count for nothing and ask, "Who am I to have an opinion of my own?"

If once you knew that you *do* count for something, that you *do* have a sound opinion of your own, that your field and factory are meant to provide for *life* and not for death, then, little man, you yourself would be able to

Who am I to have an opinion of my own?

answer the question you've just asked. You wouldn't need any diplomats. You'd stop shouting hurrah, hurrah and laying wreaths on the tomb of the Unknown Soldier. (I know your unknown soldier, little man. I got acquainted with him when I was fighting my mortal enemy in the mountains of Italy. He's the same little man as yourself, who thought he had no opinion of his own.) Instead of laying your national consciousness at the feet of your Prince Blowhard or your marshal of the world proletariat to be trampled on, you'd oppose them with *your consciousness of your own worth and your pride in your work.* You'd be able to get acquainted with your brother, the little man in Japan, China, and every other Hun country,

to give him your sound opinion of your function as a
worker, doctor, farmer, father, and husband, and convince him in the end that to make war impossible he
need only stick to his work and his love.

"That's all very well and good. But now they've made
these atom bombs. A single one of them can kill hundreds
of thousands of people!"

Use your head, little man! Do you think Prince Blowhard makes atom bombs? No, they're made by little men
who shout hurrah, hurrah instead of refusing to make
them. You see, little man, it all boils down to one thing,
to you and your sound or unsound thinking. And you,
the most brilliant scientist of the twentieth century, if
you were not a microscopically little man, you'd have
thought in terms of the world and not of any nation. Your
great intellect would have shown you how to keep the
atom bomb *out* of the world; or if the logic of scientific
development made such an invention inevitable, you'd
have brought all your influence to bear to prevent it from
being used. You're caught in a vicious circle of your own
making, and you can't get out of it because your thought
and vision have taken the wrong direction. You com-
forted millions of little men by telling them your atomic
energy would cure their cancer and rheumatism, though
you were well aware that this was impossible, that you
had devised an instrument of murder and nothing else.
You and your physics have landed in the same blind alley.
You know it, but you won't admit it. *You're finished! Now
and for all time!* I've offered you the curative powers of
my cosmic energy, little man! You know it, I've told you
so very plainly. But you keep silent, you go on dying of
cancer and a broken heart, and on your very deathbed

you cry out, "Long live culture and technology!" I tell you, little man, that you've dug your own grave with your eyes open. You think the new "era of atomic energy" has dawned. It has dawned all right, but not in the way you think. Not in your inferno but in my quiet, industrious workshop in a far corner of America.

It is entirely up to you, little man, whether or not you go to war. If you only knew that you're working for life and not for death! If you only knew that all little men on this earth are exactly like yourself, for better or worse.

Someday (how soon depends exclusively on you) you'll stop shouting hurrah, hurrah. You'll stop tilling fields and operating factories that are slated for destruction. Someday, I say, you'll no longer be willing to work for death but only for life.

"Should I declare a general strike?"

I'm not so sure. Your general strike is a poor weapon. You'll be accused—and rightly so—of letting your own women and children starve. By going on strike you will not be demonstrating your high responsibility for the weal or woe of your society. Striking is *not* working. I've told you that someday you would *work* for life, not that you'd stop working. If you insist on the word "strike," call it a "working strike." Strike by working for yourself, your children, your wife or woman, your society, your product, or your farm. Make it plain that you have no time for a war, that you have more important things to do. Outside every big city on earth, mark off a field, build high walls around it, and there let the diplomats and marshals of the earth shoot each other. That's what you could do, little man, if only you'd stop shouting hurrah, hurrah and stop believing that you're a nobody without an opinion of your own . . .

It's all in your hands, little man: not only your hammer or stethoscope but your life and your children's lives. You shake your head. You think I'm a utopian, if not a "Red."

You ask me, little man, when you will have a good, secure life. The answer is alien to your nature.

You'll have a good, secure life when being alive means more to you than security, love more than money, your freedom more than public or partisan opinion; when the mood of Beethoven's or Bach's music becomes the mood of your whole life—you have it in you, little man, somewhere deep down in a corner of your being; when your thinking is in harmony, and no longer in conflict, with your feelings; when you've learned to recognize two things in their season: your gifts and the onset of old age; when you let yourself be guided by the thoughts of great sages and no longer by the crimes of great warriors; when you cease to set more store by a marriage certificate than by love between man and woman; when you learn to recognize your errors promptly and not too late, as you do today; when you pay the men and women who teach your children better than politicians; when truths inspire you and empty formulas repel you; when you communicate with your fellow workers in foreign countries directly, and no longer through diplomats; when instead of enraging you as it does today, your adolescent daughter's happiness in love makes your heart swell with joy; when you can only shake your head at the memory of the days when small children were punished for touching their sex organs; when the human faces you see on the street are no longer drawn with grief and misery but glow with freedom, vitality, and serenity; when human bodies cease to walk this earth with rigid, retracted pelvises and frozen sex organs.

You ask for guidance and advice, little man. For thousands of years you have had guidance and advice, good and bad. Not bad advice but your own smallness is to blame for your persistent wretchedness. I could give you good advice, but in view of the way you think and are, you wouldn't be able to convert it into action for the benefit of all.

If, for instance, I advised you to put an end to all diplomacy and replace it by your professional and personal brotherhood with all the shoemakers, blacksmiths, carpenters, mechanics, engineers, physicians, educators, writers, administrators, miners, and farmers of England, Germany, Russia, the United States, Argentina, Brazil, Palestine, Arabia, Turkey, Scandinavia, Tibet, Indonesia, and so on; to let all the shoemakers in the world confer on the best way of providing the children of China with shoes; to let all the miners work out the best way of preventing human beings all over the world from suffering from cold; to let the educators of all countries and nations determine the best way of safeguarding the world's children against impotence and psychic disorder in later life; and so on. What would you do, little man, if confronted with these self-evident truths?

Assuming for the moment that you didn't have me locked up as a "Red," you would reply in person or through some spokesman of your party, church, trade union, or government:

"Who am I to replace diplomatic relations between

countries by international relations based on work and social achievement?"

Or: "There's no way of overcoming the discrepancies in the economic and social development of the various countries."

Or: "Wouldn't it be wrong to associate with the fascist Germans or Japanese, the Communist Russians, or the capitalistic Americans?"

Or: "What interests me first and foremost is my Russian, German, American, English, Jewish, or Arab fatherland."

Or: "It's all I can do to manage my own life and get along with my garment workers' union. Let someone else worry about the garment workers of other countries."

Or: "Don't listen to that capitalist, Bolshevist, fascist, Trotskyite, internationalist, sexualist, Jew, foreigner, intellectual, dreamer, utopian, fake, crank, lunatic, individualist, and anarchist! Where's your American, Russian, German, English, or Jewish patriotism?"

You would undoubtedly use one of these statements, or another of the same sort, as an excuse for shirking your responsibility for human communication.

"Am I then utterly worthless? You don't give me credit for one ounce of decency. You make hash out of me. But look here. I work hard, I support my wife and children, I try to lead a good life, I serve my country. I can't be as bad as all that!"

I know you're a decent, industrious, cooperative animal, comparable to a bee or an ant. All I've done is to lay bare the little man in you, who has been wrecking your life for thousands of years. You are *great*, little man, when you're not mean and small. Your greatness, little man, is the only hope we have left. You're great when you attend

Am I utterly worthless?

lovingly to your trade, when you take pleasure in carving and building and painting, in sowing and reaping, in the blue sky and the deer and the morning dew, in music and dancing, in your growing children, and in the beautiful body of your wife or husband; when you go to the planetarium to study the stars, to the library to read what other men and women have thought about life. You're great when your grandchild sits on your lap and you tell him of times long past and look into the uncertain future with his sweet, childlike curiosity. You're great, mother, when you lull your baby to sleep; when with tears in your eyes you pray fervently for his future happiness; and when hour after hour, year after year, you build this happiness in your child.

You're great, little man, when you sing the good, warm-hearted folk songs, or when you dance the old dances to the tune of an accordion, because folk songs are good for the soul, and they're the same the world over. And you're great when you say to your friend:

"I thank my fate that I've been able to live my life free from filth and greed, to see my children grow and to look on as they first began to babble, to take hold of things, to walk, to play, to ask questions, to laugh and to love; that I've been able to preserve, in all its freedom and purity, my feeling for the springtime and its gentle breezes, for the gurgling of the brook that flows past my house and the singing of the birds in the woods; that I've taken no part in the gossip of malicious neighbors; that I've been happy in the embrace of my wife or husband and have felt the stream of life in my body; that I haven't lost my bearings in troubled times, and that my life has had meaning and continuity. For I have always hearkened to

Yearning

the gentle voice within me that said, 'Only one thing matters: live a good, happy life. Do your heart's bidding, even when it leads you on paths that timid souls would avoid. Even when life is a torment, don't let it harden you.'"

When on quiet evenings after the day's work I sit on the meadow outside the house with my beloved or my child, alert to the breathing of nature, then a song that I love rises up in me, the song of humanity and its future: "*Seid umschlungen, Millionen . . .*" And then I implore this life to claim its rights and change the hearts of cruel or frightened men who unleash wars. They do it only because life has escaped them. And I hug my little boy, who says to me, "Father! The sun has gone away. Where has the sun gone? Will it come back soon?" And I say, "Yes, my boy, the sun will come back soon with its kindly warmth."

I have come to the end of my appeal to you, little man. I could have gone on indefinitely. But if you've read my words attentively and candidly, you will be able to recognize the little man in you even in connections I haven't mentioned. For one and the same state of mind is at the bottom of all your mean actions and thoughts.

Regardless of what you've done and will do to me, of whether you glorify me as a genius or lock me up as a madman, of whether you worship me as your deliverer or hang or torture me as a spy, your affliction will force you to recognize sooner or later that *I have discovered the laws of living energy* and have given you an instrument with which to govern your lives with the conscious purpose which thus far you have applied only to the operation of machines. I have been a faithful engineer to your organism. Your grandchildren will follow in my footsteps and become wise engineers of human nature. I have opened up to you the vast realm of the living energy within you, your cosmic essence. That is my great reward.

And to the dictators and tyrants, the crafty and malignant, the vultures and hyenas, I cry out in the words of an ancient sage:

> I have planted the banner of holy words
> in this world.
> Long after the palm tree has withered
> and the rock crumbled,
> long after the glittering monarchs
> have vanished like the dust of dried leaves,
> a thousand arks will carry my word
> through every flood:
> It will prevail.

DATE DUE

AG 30 07			
GAYLORD			PRINTED IN U.S.A